DESIGNER PHOTOSHOP

DESIGNER

PHOTO

S H O P

2ND EDITION

R O B D A Y

RANDOM HOUSE
ELECTRONIC PUBLISHING

NEW YORK

for
SAMUEL ELIOT

Copyright ©1995 by Rob Day

All rights reserved. No part of the contents of this book
may be reproduced in any form or by any means without
the written permission of the publisher.

Published in the United States by Random House, Inc.,
New York, and simultaneously in Canada by Random
House of Canada, Ltd.

Manufactured in the United States of America.

SECOND EDITION

Day, Rob.
    Designer Photoshop / by Rob Day.
        p. cm.
    Includes index.
    ISBN 0-679-74394-4
    1. Computer graphics. 2. Adobe Photoshop. I. Title.
T385.D43   1993
006.6'869—dc20   92-21201
                                      CIP

New York   Toronto   London   Sydney   Auckland

CONTENTS

ACKNOWLEDGMENTS

I am grateful to the many friends who have helped me with this book. Thanks to Claudette Moore, Cindy Ryan, Franklin Davis, Franca Taylor, Rich Day, Steve Dyer, Daniel McMullen, Mike Prendergast, and Mike Roney for their valuable suggestions. Also, thanks to Matt Brown and Steve Guttman at Adobe Systems for their excellent technical reviews.

Special thanks to Carl Sesto for teaching me about printing.

Thanks to Etienne Delessert who was very generous to take time out from his busy schedule to create beautiful artwork for my book. And also to Lance Hidy for teaching me how to use Photoshop.

And finally, thanks to Virginia Evans for her excellent design, which I am sure anyone holding this book will appreciate.

INTRODUCTION

It has been nearly six years since i had my first chance to try a beta version of Photoshop 1.0. Photoshop has matured into an extraordinary design tool, and version 3.0 bears little resemblance to that early beta program. To a beginning user, Photoshop's basic tools were immediately intuitive—a continuous-tone image could be scanned and instantly twisted, turned, skewed, and electronically painted. The program was very different from the object-oriented drawing programs I had been using, which had a very steep learning curve for making even the most rudimentary drawings. After struggling with bezier curves, Photoshop was a relief.

My enthusiasm for that early version of Photoshop was quickly tempered when I learned how difficult it would be to accurately reproduce the beautiful, glowing images that were displayed on my monitor. Again, this was the opposite of a drawing program; as cumbersome as bezier curves were to draw with, output was relatively simple—I just plugged in CMYK values that I knew would produce a desired color and printed the file.

Output becomes much more complex with Photoshop because the images are made up of thousands of colored pixels. Plugging in CMYK percentages is not an option, so the artist must have a well calibrated system and some understanding of how CMYK separations are made. There is also the issue of resolution, which is not a concern with object-oriented drawing programs. I soon learned that there is more than one kind of resolution, and that image resolution has a profound effect on the computer's performance. I also realized that the boundaries between design and production were no longer clear—in fact production skills had become part of the design process.

Because production is such an integral part of the design process when using Photoshop, I have devoted a number of chapters to these issues. In this second edition of *Designer Photoshop* the chapters relating to print production have been expanded to include color correction and sharpening techniques, plus new chapters on color management and printing with custom inks.

I have also added material relating to the upgrade from version 2.5 to 3.0, including a chapter on the new layers feature. Layers changes the nature of Photoshop by combining the advantages of an object-oriented program with a bitmap program. This feature lets you move objects within an image after they have been pasted down. In the layers chapter and others I have used step-by-step, real world projects to illustrate the program's features.

Finally, Photoshop is no longer a one-platform application. While the majority of Photoshop users are still Macintosh based, Windows users are using the program in greater numbers. Fortunately the Windows and Macintosh versions are virtually identical, making this book accessible to a Windows user even though I have made the screen captures using a Macintosh. Appendix E, *Photoshop for Windows*, outlines the few differences between the programs. No matter which system you are using, it is my sincere hope that this book will help you find your way through Photoshop's many features and improve the quality of your work.

IMAGE
BASICS

Before you start to work with Photoshop there are some elementary concepts that you should understand. Photoshop is a bitmap program which is very different from an object-oriented drawing program such as Adobe Illustrator, or page layout program such as Quark Xpress. Because it is a bitmap program, Photoshop is very good at manipulating a photograph or piece of artwork, but it is terrible at setting type. Photoshop images are displayed as as a grid of thousands of *pixels* (an acronym for picture element) so resolution and file sizes become very important issues. In this chapter I will discuss the differences in the way images are displayed on a monitor and the printed page, and the different types of resolution. Having a complete understanding of these topics will improve the quality of your Photoshop art and improve your productivity.

PRINTING PRESSES AND HALFTONE DOTS

Most black and white photographs are made up of minute silver particles suspended in a thin layer of gelatin on paper or film. The silver particles are created when light-sensitive silver halide compounds are exposed to light and chemically developed. The amount of light the compounds have been exposed to determines the density of the silver particles on the paper or film. This change in density of silver particles creates different gray values and the appearance of perfect continuous tone in a photograph (**FIGURE 1:1**).

Because printing presses are not capable of reproducing continuous tone images, most commercial printers create an illusion of continuous tone with halftone dots. Photographs and artwork are translated into rows of small, varying sized dots by an image-setter or laser printer (traditional printers use copy cameras and halftone screens). The dots create the appearance of different tones of color when they are printed. If the image is grayscale, 10 percent dots appear as light gray, 50 percent dots appear as middle gray, and so on (**FIGURE 1:2**).

 Grayscale is Photoshop's term for the translation of continuous tone photographs or artwork into different levels of gray for display on your monitor. True black and white images such as wood engravings or pen and ink drawings have no gray values, only black or white.

Printed color images are produced with a composite of four separate halftone screens set at different angles, which are transferred to printing plates. On press, the art is printed using the four plates inked with cyan, magenta, yellow, and black ink (CMYK), resulting in a wide spectrum of color. The economy of this system is obvious—running a sheet through the press hundreds of times and printing with different colored inks to reproduce a photograph or artwork would not be commercially viable (**FIGURE 1:3**).

FIGURE 1:1

Photographs are made up of minute silver particles suspended in a gelatin layer on film or paper. The particles are deposited with varying density in the gelatin layer, resulting in the appearance of continuous tone.

Printing presses are not capable of accurately reproducing the varying densities of microscopic silver particles that make up a photograph, so halftone dots are used instead.

FIGURE 1:2

STOCHASTIC SCREENING Another method of creating an appearance of continuous tone on a printed page is called stochastic screening—also known as frequency-modulated screening. Rather than modulating the size of the dots stochastic screening randomly places same-sized dots on the page. It is the distance between the dots that determines the tonality rather than the size of the dot (**FIGURE 1:4**). Stochastic has a number of advantages over halftones. Because the dots are random and there are no screen angles, there is no chance of the moiré patterns occurring that are associated with four-color halftone screening. The stochastic dot is very small, so it is capable of holding more detail than the 150 to 200 lpi halftone screens used in conventional printing. However, because the dots are so small, there is much less tolerance for error at the platemaking stage and stochastic printing will require a more skillful printer.

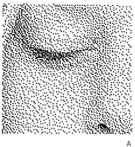

Stochastic screening (A) uses very small, randomly spaced dots. Tonality is created by altering the space between dots. Halftone screens (B) create tonality by varying the size of evenly spaced dots.

FIGURE 1:4   B

Four-color printing is a composite of four halftone screens, set at different angles, to create the illusion of many colors.

FIGURE 1:3

MONITORS AND PIXELS

Photographs and artwork are displayed on your monitor in a much different way than halftoned pictures on a printed page. A scanner scans and divides a photograph or artwork into a grid of pixels. The more pixels an image is divided into, the higher its resolution. Your monitor has an advantage over the printed page in that it can easily show thousands of colors or tones at a time. The appearance of continuous tone is created by shading each pixel with a different color, rather than changing the size of a single-colored dot. When the pixels become so small as to no longer be detected, the illusion is complete. With Photoshop, you can manipulate an electronic picture by changing the hue, value, and saturation of its pixels. Pixels can also be electronically cut and pasted within or between documents (**FIGURE 1:5**).

Hue, saturation, and value are words that describe color. Hue is a color's place along the spectrum—red, orange, yellow, green, and so on. Saturation is the brilliance of a color—the more white or black that is added to a hue, the less saturated it becomes. Value is a color's lightness or darkness, independent of hue or saturation (**FIGURE 1:6**).

DISPLAYED GRAYSCALE Your monitor displays a scan's pixels as different gray values or colors to create tonal variation within the picture; the number of values that can be displayed depends on the monitor's bit depth. One bit monitors display only two values—black and white. An 8 bit grayscale monitor can display 256 different values of gray.

Your computer assigns a code of eight 0's and 1's to each value of an 8 bit grayscale. This code is similar to Morse code, in which each letter of the alphabet is assigned a combination of dashes and dots. There are 256 possible combinations of eight 0's and 1's ($2^8 =$ 256), thus the 256 levels of gray (**FIGURE 1:7**). Only very high-end presses are capable of reproducing much more than 100 levels of gray, so the 256 values that an 8 bit grayscale monitor displays is usually more than enough information if you are working with grayscale art.

FIGURE 1:5

Computer monitors create an illusion of continuous tone with small, distinctly colored squares called pixels.

Hue

Saturation

Value

FIGURE 1:6

The top row of roses has different hues, the middle row has different saturations, and the bottom row has different values.

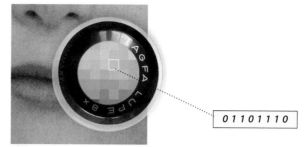

Each pixel of a grayscale image is described with 8 bits of information. The image's pixels are assigned a code of eight 0's and 1's, which determine its gray level. There are 256 possible combinations of 0's and 1's to describe 256 different values of gray.

`01101110`

FIGURE 1:7

DISPLAYED COLOR   A monitor capable of 8 bit color can display no more than 256 different colors at one time. For accurate display of color images, 256 colors are not enough, so for critical color work 24 bit color is required. A 24 bit monitor can display 256 values for each of its red, green, and blue (RGB) channels, increasing the possible number of displayed colors to 16.8 million ($2^{24} = 16,777,216$).

> **NOTE** Some monitors display 16 bit color (16,384 colors). A 16 bit color monitor configuration is less expensive than 24 bit color, and there is not too much difference in quality.

Photoshop has three color modes that are applicable to illustration and design: RGB, CMYK, and Index Color. RGB and CMYK files always contain 24 or 32 bits of information, even if your monitor's display is only 8 bit. An 8 bit display will not preview Photoshop art as accurately as a 24 bit display, but the output will be the same (**FIGURE 1:8**). You can

An 8 bit monitor (A) will not display an image as accurately as a 24 bit monitor (B), but the final output always looks the same regardless of the monitor's bit depth.

FIGURE 1:8   A   B

improve the quality of an image displayed on an 8 bit monitor by choosing Use Diffusion Dither from the General Preferences submenu under the File menu. Also, checking Use System Palette will improve Photoshop's performance with an 8 bit display (**FIGURE 1:9**). Index Color files are limited to only 256 colors when they are displayed *and* output. An Index Color file size is only one-third that of an RGB Color file, but you should not work in this mode if you want high-quality output (**FIGURE 1:10**).

Monitors and pixels are analogous to a painter's canvas and paint. To reproduce a painting in a book or magazine, usually the artist has the painting photographed and made into a transparency. The transparency is then electronically scanned and output as four color separations, which are used by a printer to make printing plates.

Photoshop art goes through a similar transformation when it is output. A Photoshop image's pixels are translated into halftone dots by an imagesetter, as are the pixels of an electronically scanned transparency (**FIGURE 1:11**). In this case, however, the artist has control over the electronic information and creates the separations as a part of the design process. The imagesetter uses the hue, saturation, and value information contained in the pixels to draw halftone dots at their proper percentages. The step of making a transparency is eliminated because the four-color separations can be generated directly from the information in the electronic file.

FIGURE 1:9

Checking Use Diffusion Dither in General Preferences will improve the preview on an 8 bit monitor.

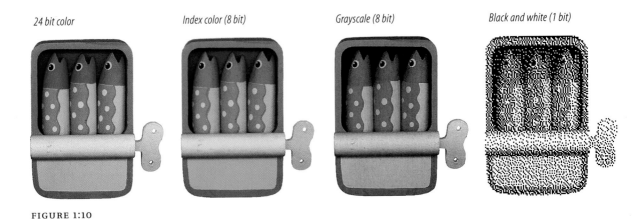

24 bit color   Index color (8 bit)   Grayscale (8 bit)   Black and white (1 bit)

FIGURE 1:10

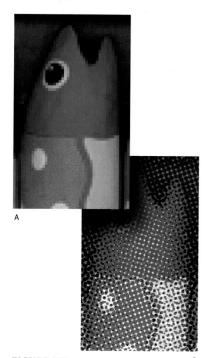

A

Electronic images are displayed on a monitor as a grid of colored pixels (A). The pixels can be millions of different hues or values, so they must be translated into halftone dots (B) if the image is to be printed economically.

FILE SIZE

The 0's and 1's that describe the pixel colors of a Photoshop image are called *bits*. The more bits that are needed to describe an image, the more space it will take up in the computer's hard drive or memory. Each image has a file size associated with it measured in kilobytes (K) or megabytes (MB). File size is determined by how many pixels an image is divided into and how many bits are used to describe each pixel (1 bit for black and white, 8 bits for grayscale, 24 bits for RGB color, and 32 bits for CMYK color). With drawing, page layout, and word processing programs, file sizes are of little concern—most files produced by these programs will easily fit on a floppy disk. Scanned images, however, often create much larger files. File size affects the speed at which your computer can manipulate an image and, in a limited way, the perceived quality of the image when it is output.

 There are 8 bits to a byte (a pixel in a grayscale image equals 1 byte). A kilobyte equals 1,024 bytes. A megabyte equals 1,024 kilobytes (1,048,576 bytes).

You can calculate the file size of any grayscale scan using the following formula:

(HEIGHT IN PIXELS X WIDTH IN PIXELS) ÷ 1,024 = FILE SIZE IN KILOBYTES

The pixels of an RGB color image are described with 24 bits (3 bytes) of information, so if the scan is RGB color, multiply the resulting file size by 3. Dividing the file size again by 1,024 gives the size in megabytes. Remember that an image's file size is determined *only* by the number of pixels that it is divided into and the pixels' bit depth, not by the image's height and width. For example, if a scan is 300 x 300 pixels, it can be output as 1 x 1 inch at 300 pixels per inch, or 10 x 10 inches at 30 pixels per inch, and the file size will not change (see **FIGURE 1:12**, *Image Size*).

FIGURE 1:12 shows that a scan with only 1 kilobyte of information does not show much detail when it is output at 2.462 x 2.462 inches. There are only 13 pixels per inch (ppi) in **FIGURE 1:12A**, and the pixels are clearly visible. To make the pixels disappear, the photograph will have to be rescanned at a much higher resolution.

Image Size

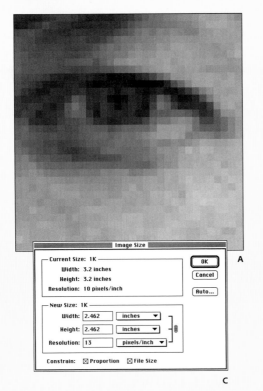

A

C

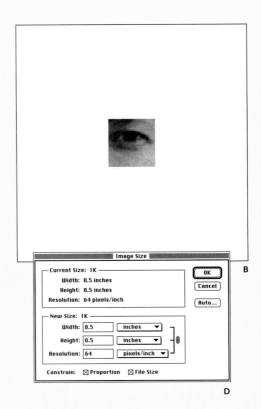

B

D

The file sizes of FIGURES A and B are the same, even though their output dimensions are different. This is because both images have the same number of pixels—1,024, making their file size 1,024 bytes or 1 kilobyte. The width and height at which an image prints out has no influence on its file size.

To manipulate an image's dimensions without changing its file size, open the Image Size dialog box (FIGURE C) under Image in Photoshop's main menu. With the Proportions and File Size boxes checked, Width, Height, and Resolution are constrained. So if Width is changed from 2.462 to 0.5 inch, Height automatically changes in proportion, from 2.462 to 0.5 inch. The resolution also changes proportionally (the size of the pixels becomes smaller) from 13 ppi to 64 ppi (FIGURE D).

RESOLUTION

Resolution can be one of the more difficult concepts to grasp when you start using Photoshop. There are three different kinds of resolution that you must be aware of, and to add to the confusion they are often referred to by one term—*dpi*. Pixels per inch (the resolution of an electronic picture), lines per inch (the halftone resolution of a printed picture), and dots per inch (the resolution of an output device) are distinctly different types of resolution, and to properly input and output images you need to know how they differ.

PIXELS PER INCH (PPI)   A scanner scans and divides artwork or a photograph into a grid of pixels that create an electronic picture (FIGURE 1:5). The pixels of the electronic picture contain the value and color information needed by an output device to translate the image into the halftone dots, which are in turn printed on the page. The more pixels an image is divided into, the higher its resolution; this kind of resolution is called pixels per inch, or ppi. If the resolution is high enough, the electronic picture will appear to have continuous tone when viewed on a monitor, and when it is output the pixels will not be visible.

Ppi is often confusingly termed *dpi*. A scanner might be referred to as scanning at 300 dpi, but in fact the scanner divides the picture into 300 pixels, not dots, per inch. The term *dpi* should be reserved for output devices to avoid confusion.

LINES PER INCH (LPI)   Printed images that use halftone dots have their own resolution, which is different from the resolution of an electronic image; this resolution is called lines per inch, or lpi (FIGURE 1:3). The lpi of a printed image is determined by how many lines of halftone dots the image is divided into. The more lines per inch, the higher the resolution. Lpi varies depending on the quality of the printing job. A newspaper uses approximately 85 lpi, a well-produced magazine may use 133 to 150 lpi, and some art books, where finer detail is desired, might be printed using 200 to 300 lpi.

DOTS PER INCH (DPI)   Dpi is the resolution of an output device. Imagesetters and laser printers output very small dots that make up the letterforms, line art, and halftone dots of a printed page. Each halftone dot is made with the even smaller imagesetter or laser printer dots; these dots are sometimes called spots or recorder elements (**FIGURE 1:13**). Most desktop laser printers print at 300 to 600 dpi, and imagesetters can output at anywhere from 1,200 to 4,000 dpi, depending on the model.

If halftone dots are to be drawn accurately with the smaller imagesetter spots, there must be an adequate enough device resolution available. A 300 dpi laser printer's most effective halftone output is at 50 to 60 lpi because there are only 300 imagesetter spots per inch available to make the halftone dots. If you attempt a higher lpi, the resulting printout will start to lose the subtle gradations of a continuous tone-image (**FIGURE 1:14**). Imagesetters must be used when you desire higher halftone frequencies. An imagesetter outputting at 2,540 dpi is capable of accurately producing 150 lpi.

MONITOR RESOLUTION   Monitor resolution adds one final element of confusion to the concept of resolution. A monitor has its own resolution that is independent of image resolution (see **FIGURE 1:15**, *The Monitor's Grid*). Most monitors have a fixed display resolution of 72 pixels per inch, which cannot be changed. With Photoshop you can specify any image resolution. Unless the image resolution is the same as, or a multiple of, the monitor's resolution, the preview displayed on the monitor is either larger or smaller than its output. Not always being able to view a picture at exactly 100 percent takes some getting used to, but the ability to work with any image resolution is worth the inconvenience.

Halftone dots are made up of even smaller imagesetter or laser printer dots.

FIGURE 1:13

FIGURE 1:14   A   B

Each halftone dot is made with smaller imagesetter spots. If you specify a halftone screen that is too high for the output device, the result will be fewer possible gray levels in the printed piece. Figure A was output at 150 lpi from a 300 dpi laser printer. Figure B shows the results when the same file is output at 53 lpi from a 300 dpi laser printer.

The Monitor's Grid

Photoshop allows you to work at any image resolution. However, your monitor has a fixed resolution that is independent of the image's resolution; most monitors have resolutions of 72 pixels per inch. For display purposes, an image that does not conform to the grid of the monitor is increased or decreased in size.

FIGURE A shows how an image that is 6 x 6 inches and 100 ppi would look against a 19-inch monitor's grid. When the image is displayed, it conforms to the 72 ppi of the monitor and appears as 8.33 x 8.33 inches (FIGURE B). The output dimensions are still 6 x 6 inches even though the display dimensions are larger.

A

B

IMAGE QUALITY

The quality of a printed image can be altered in many ways during the production process whether you work traditionally or electronically. The tendency for many users is to overemphasize the importance of image resolution and ignore other factors that may affect a finished print. Below is a brief description of the production operations that will have an impact on the final print quality when you work with Photoshop. Most of these operations are covered in greater detail later in the book. Some are more important than others, and depending on time and budget constraints, you may decide to cut corners; if you don't, however, the resulting quality will match most traditional color work.

QUALITY OF THE ORIGINAL Photoshop's ability to improve the quality of a mediocre original is remarkable. However, there is a limit to how much can be done to improve a photograph that is out of focus or has poor tonal range. So, unless you are using a bad photograph for artistic effect, pay attention to the quality of the original art.

THE SCANNER Scanners differ in capability and price. A $1,200 flatbed scanner cannot match the dynamic range or production capabilities of an $80,000 drum scanner—which is not to say an inexpensive scanner is useless. For the price, a flatbed scanner may be the best piece of hardware you can buy. With some time and skillful color correction, commercially acceptable output is possible with a desktop scanner (see FIGURE 8:13, *Comparing Scanners*). The convenience of the flatbed scanner lends itself to the creative process, and if you are heavily manipulating images, or the final printing will not be the highest possible quality, a perfect scan may not be necessary. Flatbeds also have the advantage of being able to scan three-dimensional objects. If, on the other hand, you require precise color correction and accurate reproduction of high-quality transparencies, and don't want to spend much time color correcting, you should purchase scans from trade shops or service bureaus that use high-end scanners.

COLOR MANAGEMENT   Photoshop has a very sophisticated color management system designed to give you WYSWYG (what you see is what you get) color, which, if used properly, can reasonably match the output from most printing devices to most displays. As soon as you manipulate an image with Photoshop the color of the artwork becomes "synthetic"—the artwork exists only as it is displayed on a monitor. Unfortunately, different monitors often display color differently. This means that your service bureau or trade shop may not have an accurate visual reference to your artwork. Designers have avoided this problem when using page layout or drawing programs by simply inserting CMYK percentages to create a desired color, rather than trusting what they see on their monitors. This strategy is not practical with Photoshop images because they contain thousands of different colors. Unless you are very familiar with how CMYK values will print under different conditions, then you must be able to calibrate and rely on your display when using Photoshop (see Chapter Fifteen, *Color Management*).

IMAGE RESOLUTION   The resolution of a scan, measured in pixels per inch, has a profound effect on the quality of output. However, scanning at the highest possible resolution and creating huge files does not necessarily ensure high-quality output. Keep in mind that the ultimate resolution of any printed image is the halftone dot. The pixels of an electronic picture carry the information an imagesetter needs to make the halftone dots. Beyond a certain point—usually between one and two pixels per halftone dot—there is a diminishing return of quality. More than two pixels per halftone dot most often is wasted information.

Using the correct resolution is important because the image's resolution determines its file size, and file size affects the speed of your computer's operation. Doubling ppi quadruples file size. The larger the file size, the slower your computer will operate, and the longer the imagesetter will take to output the file.

SHARPENING   Most scans need to be sharpened. A high-end scanner sharpens an image using its own software. Desktop scanners may have options for sharpening in their softwares, but usually the controls are not very sophisticated. Photoshop's Unsharp Mask filter allows the user to sharpen an image in a myriad of ways depending on the type of image and the user's taste (see Chapter Seven, *Sharpening*).

THE HALFTONE SCREEN   It is easy to become too concerned with image resolution and forget about the halftone dot, which is the ultimate resolution of a printed piece. Printers usually use 133 or 150 lpi, and at these screen frequencies it is possible to detect the halftone patterns with the naked eye. Printing presses have limits, so halftone screens are restricted to a relatively low resolution. There are printers who can handle 200 to 300 line halftones, but be prepared to pay a high price for this service. (See **FIGURE 1:16**, *Comparing Halftone Screens*.)

CONVERTING RGB TO CMYK   RGB color is called additive color. Red, green, and blue (RGB) are the primary colors of your monitor and are added together to make white. Cyan, magenta, and yellow (CMY) are the primary colors of the printing press and they are referred to as subtractive colors. When mixed together at 100 percent the CMY pigments subtract or absorb light resulting in dark brown (see FIGURE 15:2, *RGB and CMYK Color*). Unfortunately, in printing, you cannot make black by combining these three colors, so a fourth color—black (or the key color)—must be added. A conversion must be made from RGB color to CMYK color before an image can be printed.

There are many options available in Photoshop for making the conversion from RGB to CMYK that affect the quality of a printed piece. Translating the electronic image from RGB color to CMYK color can have the greatest impact on quality. Not only does Photoshop's color management occur in the translation, but the important black generation also occurs during the conversion (see Chapter Fifteen, *Color Management*).

IMAGESETTERS   Separations for final artwork are output on an imagesetter at a service bureau or color trade shop. Imagesetters output high-resolution film separations, which are used to expose the printing plate. However, imagesetters vary in capability. Make sure that color separations are made by an output device that was designed for multicolor work. The Linotronic 300, for example, is capable of making color separations, but it was designed for one-color work, so the separations may not register well. The Linotronic 330 is a better choice because it was designed for producing accurate color separations.

Comparing Halftone Screens

Halftone screen frequency, measured in lines per inch, is the resolution of printed images. The importance of the halftone screen's relationship to image quality is often overlooked. Most commercial printers are limited to 150 lpi.

An effective way to increase the detail in a printed picture is to use a finer halftone screen, but higher screen frequencies require skillful printing. Few commercial printers print with halftone resolutions of more than 200 lpi, and those that can will most likely be more expensive. FIGURES A, B, and C all have the same image resolution—300 ppi—but have different halftone resolutions. FIGURE A is screened at 85 lpi, FIGURE B at 120 lpi, and FIGURE C at 150 lpi.

85 lpi   A

120 lpi   B

150 lpi   C

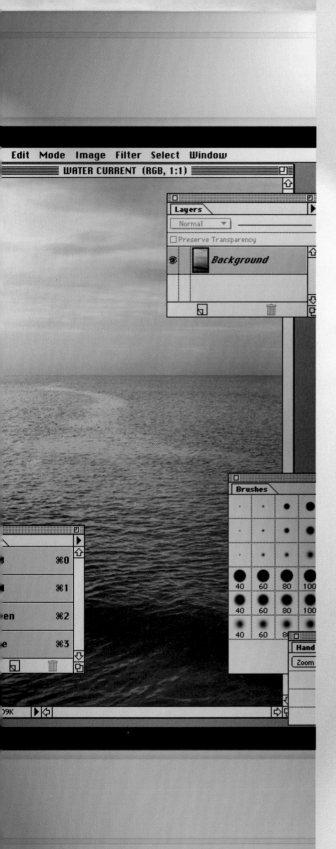

WORKING CONDITIONS 2

Pʜᴏᴛᴏsʜᴏᴘ ʜᴀs ᴀɴ ᴀʀʀᴀʏ ᴏғ ᴛᴏᴏʟs designed to let you adjust a picture's tonality and color. How you set up your work space plays a surprisingly important role in the accuracy of any adjustments you make based on what you see on your display. A work space's ambient light, and the adjustments you might make to your monitor have little importance if you are word processing or typesetting. However, the appearance of displayed Photoshop images will change depending on these conditions, even though the digital values that describe them stay the same. Understanding how the working environment and display change your perception of an image is essential for accurate output.

This chapter covers how to control the ambient light of your workspace and adjust the brightness (sometimes referred to as gamma) and color-cast (or white point temperature) of a monitor. Stabilizing your viewing conditions is only part of getting what you see on to the printed page—it is also important to manage color as it is sent to different output devices and that will be covered in Chapter Fifteen, *Color Management*.

STABLE VIEWING CONDITIONS

The output from a professionally run service bureau or trade shop always remains consistent—if you send the same file to the same output device more than once, the output should look the same each time the file is run. An imagesetter needs constant attention to maintain consistent output, and this consistency is critical if you are to have any chance of matching output to your display. Conversely, your monitor should always display the same image consistently. Ensuring that the ambient light and monitor settings are stable will allow you to manage color more accurately.

GAMMA AND WHITE POINT

You may have noticed that the televisions in a retail showroom all display color in a slightly different way; they vary in saturation and warmth or coolness of color. Computer displays have a similar problem. A file will rarely look exactly the same on different monitors, even if the monitors are manufactured by the same company.

A number of monitor manufacturers make hardware calibrators that allow you to change the gamma and white point temperature of a monitor. The calibrator allows you to set your monitor to a standard that can be duplicated over time, adjusting for factors such as heat and humidity and the monitor's age. The device is usually a sensor that attaches to the face of your display with a suction cup; the sensor reads a test pattern of the monitor's red, green, and blue values, and adjusts the display for any deficiencies (**FIGURE 2:1**). If you use a hardware calibrator, you should calibrate your display about once a month. It is important to understand that calibrators do not guarantee a color match to any specific output device; their only purpose is to stabilize your display over time. Color matching to a specific device is done via Photoshop's Printing Inks and Monitors preferences files (see Chapter Fifteen, *Color Management*).

GAMMA CONTROL PANEL SOFTWARE Adobe provides a software calibrator with the Macintosh version of Photoshop that allows you to adjust a display's gamma and white point. This utility is very useful if you cannot justify the added expense of a hardware calibrator. On the disk labeled Calibration disk, there is a control panel device named Gamma. Make sure that you put Gamma into your system's control panel folder (Windows users see Appendix E, *Photoshop for Windows*).

Gamma is very easy and intuitive to use (see your Photoshop User Guide for detailed instructions). It allows you to change the gamma and color balance of your display interactively (**FIGURE 2:2**). The disadvantage of Gamma is that it cannot adjust for slight changes that might occur due to aging of the monitor or surrounding heat and humidity. Once you have settled on the gamma and color temperature for your display, you should not change them, so that what you see on screen will be consistent from one working session to the next.

WHITE POINT TEMPERATURE The perceived warmth or coolness of white on your display is measured in degrees Kelvin. White on many uncalibrated displays can have a cool blue cast that resembles 10 to 15 percent cyan, which is very difficult to compensate for in your output. Some monitor manufacturers have started shipping monitors with a white point temperature of between 5000°K and 6500°K, which is more appropriate for print applications. Adjusting the monitor's temperature to between 5000°K and 6500°K displays white as the approximate color of white paper viewed in daylight (**FIGURE 2:3**).

Figure A shows a monitor set at 5000°K, which is an appropriate setting for print-related use. Figure B shows an uncalibrated monitor with a blue cast that resembles 15% cyan.

FIGURE 2:3

FIGURE 2:2

Knoll Software's Gamma control panel is a software calibrator. The control panel lets you set the gamma, black, and white points of your display.

GAMMA The lightness or darkness of your display, adjusted for the way we perceive values, is called *gamma*. Computers display the grayscale in an evenly distributed way, while our eyes compress the dark and light ends of the grayscale so that we see images in higher contrast. Adjusting the gamma is a way to alter a monitor's middle tones relative to the way we see (**FIGURE 2:4**). A gamma setting of between 1.8 and 2.0 is appropriate for output to print (**FIGURE 2:5**).

 It is very important to note that the Gamma setting listed in Photoshop's Monitor Setup under the Preference menu has a different function from the Gamma Control Panel software that ships with the Macintosh version of Photoshop. The Monitor preference is not used to set the gamma of your display. This setting tells the program how you have adjusted the actual gamma of your display using either a hardware calibrator or the Gamma Control Panel. The Monitor Setup preference compensates for a variety of displays and viewing conditions when you convert an image from RGB to CMYK Mode (see Chapter Fifteen, *Color Management*).

MONITOR CONTROLS Your monitor also most likely has hardware controls for adjusting brightness and contrast of the display. Because you want to be sure that the display is consistent over time, you should decide what settings you prefer and then tape down the controls. This will ensure that the display is not inadvertently adjusted (**FIGURE 2:6**).

A

B

FIGURE 2:4   C

Figure B shows how an image becomes less contrasted when its values are lightened uniformly (by 10 percent in this case). If the values are adjusted on a curve where the middle values are adjusted more than the highlights and shadows (C), the result accurately reflects the way we see. The curve is called gamma.

Figure A shows a calibrated display set at 5000°K and 1.2 gamma. Figure B shows a calibrated display set at 5000°K and 2.0 gamma.

A

B

FIGURE 2:5

AMBIENT LIGHT

The impact that the surrounding light has on a displayed image is not immediately obvious to a new Photoshop user. It is easy to experience this effect by displaying an image with the room darkened, and then turning on the overhead lights and observing how the image changes. The bright overhead lights make the image shadows look lighter and the colors duller (**FIGURE 2:7**). If you were to color-correct the image one day with the overhead lights on and the next day with them off, your color correction would be very inconsistent. If there are windows in your space, then changes in ambient light occur gradually and you may not notice the shift. The ideal work space is a windowless room with lighting that does not reflect off the monitor's display.

It is also important to have a 5000°K light source to illuminate target prints from different output devices. The targets are used for managing the color of an image when it is printed from a variety of output devices (see Chapter Fifteen, *Color Management*).

Make sure that once you set your monitor's brightness/contrast controls that you tape them down so that they are not inadvertently moved.

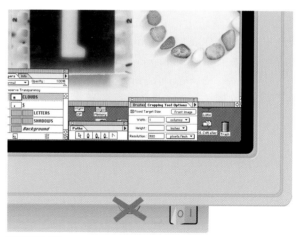

FIGURE 2:6

A display's color will vary depending on the surrounding light. If the overhead lighting is bright, then an image's shadows will look lighter and colors will look duller (A). It is best to have moderate to low ambient light with no overhead lights (B).

FIGURE 2:7   A   B

The 5000°K light is neutral, without either a blue or yellow cast that will come from either fluorescent or incandescent lights. The light source does not need to be elaborate; it can be a simple fluorescent fixture with a 5000°K bulb (Sylvania makes a bulb called DESIGN 50 that is rated at 5000°K). I built a viewing booth for my studio out of Fome Core that cost less than $35 (see **FIGURE 2:8**, *Building a 5000°K Light Booth*).

 If you work in a group environment where it is impossible to control the ambient light, then an attempt should be made to establish one work station in an area where the light can be controlled. All final color decisions and RGB-TO-CMYK conversions should be made on that work station.

Building a 5000°K Light Booth

It is very important to control the the ambient light of your studio. Usually you will want to keep the lighting very low so that there is no glare off your display. To accurately manage color, you will need to make adjustments to Photoshop's Printing Inks Setup based on a target print output from a variety of devices (see Chapter Fifteen, *Color Management*). The output target ideally should be illuminated with a 5000°K light source behind your monitor so that no color casts from other light sources influence your judgment of the target (FIGURE A). A simple booth can be constructed for a 24-inch fluorescent strip light out of Fome Core or corrugated cardboard. FIGURE B shows a drawing for a booth that I constructed for my studio.

A

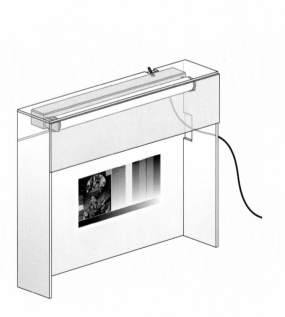

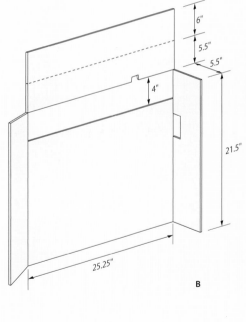

6"

5.5"

5.5"

4"

21.5"

25.25"

B

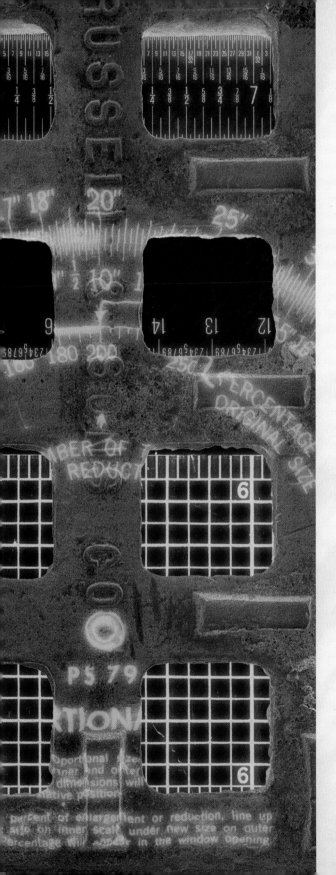

3

RULERS
AND
RATIOS

Photoshop PROVIDES A NUMBER OF
tools that will aid you in accurately judging
an image's detail, print dimensions, and
file size before it is output. These tools are
needed because your monitor's resolution
is fixed, while an image's resolution can be
whatever you desire (see FIGURE 1:15, *The
Monitor's Grid*). It is unusual that an
image's on-screen dimensions will match
its output dimensions (unless you want to
work at an image resolution that equals
your monitor's, usually 72 pixels per inch).
Also, as you zoom in and out of an image,
its preview can be slightly distorted, so it is
important to make critical judgments at
the correct magnification.

These handicaps are overcome to some degree by the Photoshop interface, which gives you visual clues about the actual output dimensions and image quality. This chapter covers the tools and elements of the Photoshop interface that are designed to let you navigate around a picture and make accurate on-screen judgments about the image quality before it is output.

ZOOM AND HAND TOOLS

You can zoom in and out of an image using the Zoom tool. It is easy when you are starting to use Photoshop, to confuse zooming in and out with physically resizing an image for output. The zoom tool simply lets you examine an image more closely and has no effect on a picture's dimensions when you print.

To magnify an image without changing the window's size, select the Zoom tool and click inside of the image's window. Holding down the option key while you click zooms the image back out. If another tool is selected, holding down the Command+Spacebar and clicking zooms in, while adding the option key lets you zoom out.

You can also choose Zoom In (Command++) or Zoom Out (Command+-) from the Window menu. Choosing Zoom In or Zoom Out is subtly different from using the Zoom tool in that, if you haven't adjusted the window's shape, by clicking and dragging on the window's lower right-hand size box, the window will expand or contract along with the image. If you have adjusted the window shape, it will remain that way until you click the window's zoom box; now when you type Command++ or Command+-, the window will expand or collapse with the image. If you want to reduce or expand the preview without changing the window's size, move back to using the Zoom tool. Typing the letter Z is a shortcut for selecting the Zoom tool.

 If you want to quickly zoom in on a specific part of an image, click and drag when the Zoom tool is selected (Command + Spacebar), and a marquee will appear. Drag the marquee to surround the part of the image on which you want to zoom in. When you release the mouse button, the image area inside of the marquee will fill the window. Also, if you want to zoom in to the maximum magnification, press Command + Option + +. Pressing Command + Option + – zooms out to the minimum magnification.

If an image's pixel dimensions are higher then your monitor's, you can only view part of the image when the ratio is 1:1.

FIGURE 3:1

With the monitor pixel to image pixel ratio at 6:1, you can clearly see the individual pixels of the image.

FIGURE 3:2

HAND TOOL   You can scroll through an image that has overflowed its window by clicking and dragging on the window's scroll bars. You can also click on the Hand tool and then click and drag inside the window to move the image. Holding down the Spacebar accesses the Hand tool if another tool is selected. Typing the letter H is also a shortcut for selecting the Hand tool.

MONITOR PIXEL TO IMAGE PIXEL RATIO

In the titlebar of every Photoshop file there is a ratio number. The ratio indicates how many monitor pixels are used to preview the pixels of an image. As you zoom in and out of an image you will notice that the titlebar's ratio changes. The ratio is important because it lets you know if you are viewing the image's detail in its entirety. For example, if the ratio is 1:1, then you know that every image pixel is being displayed using one monitor pixel, and you are seeing all of the picture's detail. If the image has a fairly high resolution (its pixel dimensions are higher than your monitor's), then you can only view part of the image at this ratio (**FIGURE 3:1**). Zooming in even closer, to a ratio of 6:1, for example, means that 6 monitor pixels are describing every image pixel. Now you can start to see the image pixels clearly (**FIGURE 3:2**).

If you zoom back out so that the ratio is less than 1:1, then more than one image pixel is described with one monitor pixel. At a ratio of 1:4 the preview is adjusted so that 4 image pixels are previewed with one monitor pixel. In this case the preview is slightly distorted and can be deceiving. An image that has been correctly sharpened will look unpleasantly noisy if the ratio is less than 1:1, but it will look correct when it is printed. Also, there can be unwanted artifacts in an image that will be visible at 1:1 but not evident at a lower ratio (**FIGURE 3:3**). This ratio is very important when making judgments about details of an image.

It is important to make critical judgments at a 1:1 ratio. The 1 pixel wide, horizontal white lines on the T in Figure A show at a 1:1 ratio, but not at a 1:2 ratio (B).

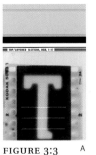 

FIGURE 3:3   A   B

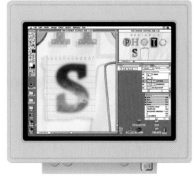

Having a second pre-view window zoomed out while you work on the image at 1:1 allows you to work on a detail of the picture in one window and still see the entire image in the other.

FIGURE 3:4

 Double-clicking the Zoom Tool instantly sizes a preview to a 1:1 ratio. Double-clicking the Hand tool instantly sizes the preview so that it displays the entire image with its window collapsed, as largely as possible within your monitor's display area.

CREATING AN EXTRA PREVIEW WINDOW If you are working on a high-resolution image and want to edit at a 1:1 ratio and still see the entire picture, you can create a duplicate window. While you work at a 1:1 ratio or higher in one window, the other window can be zoomed out, so that it is fully visible (**FIGURE 3:4**). Choose New Window from the Window menu to make an extra preview of the image you are working on. When you choose New Window, any changes you make will be updated in both windows. New Window only duplicates the preview, not the actual file.

FILE SIZE INDICATOR In the lower left corner of every Photoshop image's window is a file size indicator. There are two file sizes given. The first number shows the file size of the image as a single layered document with no extra channels, or as it would be sent to a printer, and the second shows the file size including any extra layers or channels. (Layers is a new Photoshop 3.0 feature that allows you to assign parts of the image to different layers, making them easier to move. See Chapter Twelve, *Layers.*) You can also click on the arrow next to the file size indicator and choose Scratch Sizes. In this case the left number indicates the amount of RAM and scratch disk space being used by all open documents, and the second indicates the amount of RAM available to Photoshop. The program itself takes about 9 MB of RAM, so if you have applied 35 MB to Photoshop, then 26 MB will show in the scratch disk indicator. (See Appendix C, *Faster Photoshop.*)

If you click on the lower left corner, you get a pop-up icon representing the image's relationship to the page size. The size and orientation of the page icon are determined by the settings in Page Setup under the File menu. Clicking on the lower left corner with the Option key pressed gives you more information on the picture—its dimensions both in pixels and whatever measurement units are being used, the number of channels, and its resolution (**FIGURE 3:5**).

RULERS You can also choose Show Rulers (Command+R) from the Window menu. Rulers will appear on the left and upper sides of the window. Clicking and dragging from the upper left corner of the rules lets you set the zero coordinates of the rulers to any-

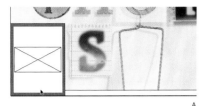

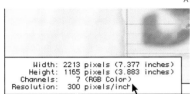

Width: 2213 pixels (7.377 inches)
Height: 1165 pixels (3.883 inches)
Channels: 7 (RGB Color)
Resolution: 300 pixels/inch

FIGURE 3:5

Clicking on the file size indicator at a window's lower left-hand corner causes a pop-up icon to show which indicates the file's printed dimensions relative to the page (A). Holding down the option key and clicking gives more file info (B).

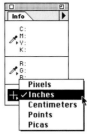

FIGURE 3:6

Clicking on the small arrow at the bottom of the Info palette lets you quickly choose the units displayed by the rulers.

where inside the window. Double-clicking the ruler's upper left corner resets the zero coordinates to the upper left of the image.

If you choose Show Info from the Palettes submenu under Window, you can see a digital readout of your mouse position as it appears inside of the window. The readout appears at the bottom of the Info palette; clicking on the small arrow lets you change the ruler units to Pixels, Inches, Points, Picas or Centimeters (**FIGURE 3:6**). The ruler units can also be changed by choosing Units from the Preferences submenu under Window.

BACKGROUND VIEWS   If the clutter of your desktop becomes distracting you can quickly hide it by clicking on the middle or far-right icon at the very bottom of the Toolbox. The left icon is the default and shows the entire desktop. Clicking on the middle icon previews the active Photoshop window on a gray background along with the Menu bar, Tool box, and any open palettes. Clicking on the right-hand icon previews the active Photoshop window on a black background and hides the Menu bar (**FIGURE 3:7**). Typing the letter F is a shortcut for changing the background mode. Typing F again cycles through the three modes.

A

Clicking on the three icons at the bottom of the tool box lets you show the active window normally (A), on a gray background hiding other windows (B), or a black background (C).

B

C

FIGURE 3:7

The Commands Palette

The Commands palette is new with Photoshop 3.0. Version 2.5 allowed you to set a preference file that assigned the F-keys on extended keyboards to menu items that did not have key command shortcuts. The new Commands palette lets you use these shortcuts even if you do not have an extended keyboard—clicking on the menu item in the palette chooses that item from Photoshop's menu.

You can customize the Commands palette to suit your needs. Click on the arrow in the palette's upper right corner and choose Edit Commands from the pop-up menu (FIGURE A). The Edit Commands menu shows a list of menu items currently included in the palette. You can delete an item by clicking on it, and then clicking the Delete key. To add an item, click New, and choose any menu or submenu item from the Photoshop menu bar; you can then color-code the new item by choosing a color from the Color pop-up menu, or assign it an F-key from the Function Key pop-up menu (FIGURE B). You can also rearrange the placement of items in the palette by clicking on their names and dragging them to a new position in the Edit Commands dialog. If you want the palette to have a different shape, change the Columns number—I use 9 so that my palette stretches across the bottom of the screen (FIGURE C).

A

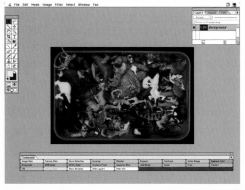

B

C

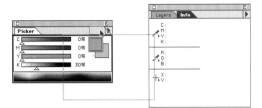

FIGURE 3:9

You can create any grouping of the palettes by dragging and dropping one palette into another.

Each palette has a menu which can be accessed by clicking on the arrow in the palette's upper right-hand corner.

FIGURE 3:10

You can hide the tool box and any floating palettes by pressing the Tab key. This can be useful if you are using one tool for an extended period. Pressing the Tab key again brings the Tool box and Palettes back into view. If you are using the Pen tool your path will disappear along with the palettes; type the letter T after pressing the Tab key to get your path back.

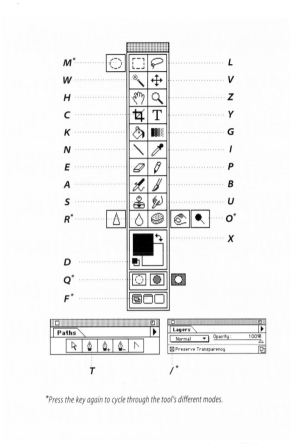

*Press the key again to cycle through the tool's different modes.

FIGURE 3:11

Press any letter on your keyboard (with the exception of J) to activate one of Photoshop's tools.

PALETTES   Some of Photoshop's tools reside in floating palettes, which can be opened or closed and arranged depending on your needs. To show or hide a palette choose it from the Palettes submenu under Window. Photoshop 3.0 has added three new palettes—Layers, Options, and Commands (see **FIGURE 3:8**, *The Commands Palette*), and what was the Colors palette in version 2.5 has been split into the Picker, Swatches, and Scratch palettes.

Version 3.0 also allows you to arrange the palettes into groups of any combination. When palettes are grouped their titles appear on nested tabs—clicking on a title makes that palette active. To split or combine the palettes, click and drag on the title of the palette you want to move and drag it to a new palette (**FIGURE 3:9**). Each palette has more menu items that can be accessed by clicking and dragging on the arrow in its upper right-hand corner (**FIGURE 3:10**).

With Photoshop 3.0, pressing any of the keyboard letters has an effect on the interface. For instance, you can press the letter A and the Airbrush is selected in the toolbox; press the E and the Eraser is selected, and so on. **FIGURE 3:11** diagrams the keyboard shortcuts.

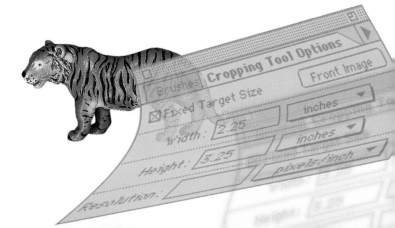

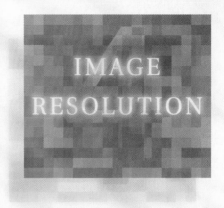

IMAGE RESOLUTION

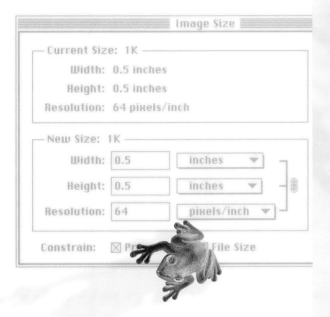

WHEN YOU WORK WITH BITMAPPED images in a program such as Photoshop, you must choose an image resolution. This is an important decision because image resolution affects output quality and file size. The more pixels into which an image is divided, the longer it will take a computer to perform operations. File sizes that you can work with are limited by the processing power of your computer and the available disk and memory space (see **FIGURE 4:1**, *Resolution and File Size*).

There is a general rule-of-thumb for choosing an image resolution—the *Photoshop User Guide* suggests an image resolution of two pixels for every one halftone dot—for instance, if the lpi is 150, then the ppi should be 300. This rule normally provides enough resolution to make any image appear fully resolved when it is printed with high-end presses. Different images, however, can need more or less resolution—soft-edged pictures don't need the same amount of resolution as pictures with high contrast and fine details. You may also decide that you are willing to sacrifice some subtle details in the name of making the file size more manageable.

The first step in choosing image resolution is to know what the lpi of the printed piece will be. If you decide to strictly adhere to the two pixels to one halftone dot ratio, the file size may become too large for many computers to handle. For instance, a 4 × 5 inch RGB scan at 300 ppi is 5.15 MB; if the dimensions were 8 × 10 inch, its file size would be 20.6 MB. Keeping the image resolution as low as possible while still maintaining image detail is very important for productivity (see **FIGURE 4:2**, *The 2:1 Ratio*). Also, Photoshop 3.0 file sizes will be potentially larger because the new Layers feature allows you to have multiple layers in one file, all of which take additional space. (See Chapter Twelve, *Layers*)

In many cases the 2:1 ratio is more resolution than is necessary. You will see very little degradation of image detail when the ratio is lowered to 1½:1 (see **FIGURE 4:3**, *Comparing Image Resolutions*). The 8 × 10 inch color scan at 225 ppi changes from 20.6 to 11.6 MB.

FIGURE 4:1

Resolution and File Size

This graph shows how file size changes as the ppi is increased in an 8 × 10 inch RGB Color image. Notice that the file size at 150 ppi is about 5 megabytes. If the resolution is doubled to 300 ppi, the file size quadruples to 20 megabytes.

Unless your computer is fast and equipped with at least 80 MB of memory, it will be difficult to seriously manipulate this 20 MB file. By lowering the resolution of the image from 300 to 200 ppi, which would have little effect on its quality (see FIGURE 4:3, *Comparing Image Resolutions*), the file size changes to about 9 MB. Although some operations might still be slow, this file size is much more manageable.

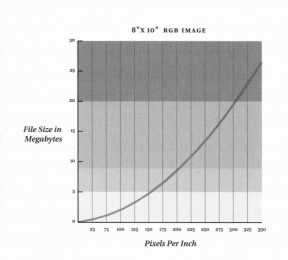

8"x 10" RGB IMAGE

File Size in Megabytes

Pixels Per Inch

The 2:1 Ratio

When you choose an image resolution, keep in mind that the 2:1 image to halftone dot ratio is only a rule-of-thumb. As you can see from FIG-URE 4:3, *Comparing Image Resolutions*, the changes in image detail between different resolutions can be quite subtle, and in the case of soft images, almost nonexistent. Here are some situations that require more or less resolution:

- **FINE LINES:** There are some occasions where a 2:1, or even higher, ratio is useful. Any image that has delicate fine lines in high contrast to the background, as in FIGURES A–C, might benefit from higher resolution. The image resolution in FIGURE A is 225 ppi; FIGURE B is 300 ppi; and FIGURE C is 500 ppi.

- **SOFT EDGES:** There must be an edge to define for high resolution to be meaningful. The clouds in FIGURE 4:3 don't require as much resolution as the etching on this page.

- **VIEWING DISTANCE:** Consider the distance from which the printed piece will be viewed. The resolving power of our eyes is limited, so if you are designing a poster or billboard, the viewer will stand away from the poster and not be able to resolve much image detail. If you think you can discern a difference between the images in FIGURE 4:3 at a normal reading distance, hold the page 3 to 4 feet away and see if you still can see differences.

225 ppi　　　　　　　　　　　A

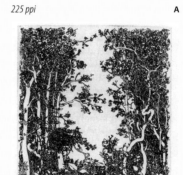

300 ppi　　　　　　　　　　　B

500 ppi　　　　　　　　　　　C

© 1967 LANCE HIDY

Comparing Image Resolutions

300 pixels per inch, 1,750 kilobytes   **A**   *225 pixels per inch, 1,011 kilobytes*   **B**

Above are two different kinds of pictures scanned at various resolutions. The landscape has fine detail and hard edges, while the clouds have mostly soft edges. All of the pictures have a halftone resolution of 150 lpi. The pictures in columns A–C are 300, 225, and 150 ppi respectively.

The details of the pictures in column C are not as sharply defined as the pictures in the other columns. This degradation in detail is more noticeable in pictures with sharp edges, like the landscape. The change in image detail is subtle, though, and for many applications this level of detail is acceptable, particularly if

150 pixels per inch, 450 kilobytes   C

150 pixels per inch with unsharp mask applied   D

the image is soft-edged, like the clouds. Any difference in picture detail between columns A and B is barely perceptible, even though the file size of column A's pictures is nearly twice that of column B's. Column D's pictures are 150 ppi with Photoshop's Unsharp Mask filter applied. The Unsharp Mask Amount was set at

250%, the Radius set at 0.5 pixels, and the Threshold set at 1. Skillfully applied unsharp masking can give the illusion of more image detail at lower resolutions. (See Chapter Seven, *Sharpening*.)

Lowering the ratio to 1:1 causes a slightly more noticeable degradation of image quality, but for some images this level of quality is acceptable. If the image is very detailed with hard edges, such as the texture of rock or the spokes of a bicycle wheel, you may detect a loss in detail, but if the image has soft edges, such as clouds, the change is less noticeable. The 8 × 10 inch scan at 150 ppi is now 5.15 MB, at 4 × 5 inch the 150 ppi scan is only 1.29 MB.

 The above discussion of image resolution applies to grayscale and color art only. Black and white art—that is, an image in Bitmap mode under Photoshop's Mode menu—needs a much higher resolution. If there are no gray values in an image then there will be no halftone dots. A black and white only image is defined by the imagesetter's spots (dpi) rather than the coarser halftone screen. A higher resolution is needed to accurately define the edges of pure black on white. Black and white images should have a resolution of between 800 and 1,200 ppi if they are to be accurately output from a high-resolution imagesetter (**FIGURE 4:4**). Bitmapped images contain only one bit of information per pixel, so they are one-eighth the size of a grayscale image with the same resolution.

RESIZING AND RESAMPLING

You can manipulate both the print dimensions and pixel dimensions of an image via the Image Size dialog box found in the Image menu. As I mentioned in Chapter One, the physical dimensions at which a picture will print has no bearing on its file size—it is the pixel dimensions that determine file size. When you

Black and white images (Bitmap Mode) need higher resolutions. Here are three black and white only images at different resolutions. Figure A is 150 ppi, figure B is 300 ppi, and figure C is 800 ppi.

A

B

© 1970 LANCE HIDY

FIGURE 4:4   C

have both the Proportions and File Size boxes checked in the Image Size dialog box, you can change the print dimensions without changing the file size—the size of the pixels are expanded or contracted as you change the print dimensions (see FIGURE 1:12, *Image Size*).

There are many cases in which you may want to change the print dimensions while maintaining the image resolution or adjust the image resolution while maintaining the print dimensions—this is called re-sampling. In this case Photoshop is either adding or subtracting pixels to the image. Uncheck the File Size box in the Image Size dialog to resample an image (see FIGURE 4:5, *Changing Image Resolutions*). Unchecking both Proportions and File Size means that you can adjust one dimension without proportionally constraining the other—in this case the image will be distorted.

 If you make a mistake entering dimensions in the Image Size dialog box you can hold down the Option key, which converts the Cancel button to a Reset button. Clicking Reset converts the dialog to the way it was when you opened it.

INTERPOLATION When you resample an image either by increasing or decreasing its pixel dimensions, Photoshop must interpolate how to add or subtract pixels. You can specify an interpolation method by clicking on the Interpolation pop-up menu found in the General Preferences submenu under the file menu. You have three choices: Nearest Neighbor, Bilinear, or Bicubic. Bicubic is the default and is generally the method that should be used because it is the most accurate for a continuous tone image. There are some occasions where Nearest Neighbor should be used (see Chapter Nine, *The Creative Pixel*).

CANVAS SIZE Often you will want to add to the available work space (increase the canvas size) of an image. Choose Canvas Size from the Image menu to get the Canvas Size dialog box. This dialog allows you to add any number of pixels to the existing work area. You can increase the width and height of the image by typing new dimensions in the Width and Height boxes; clicking on the grid next to Placement determines to which side of the page the pixels will be added. The shaded block represents the page as it exists before the change in canvas size. If the middle block is shaded then the pixels are added on all four sides of the image; if the lower-right block is shaded then the pixels are added to the top and left of the image and; so on (**FIGURE 4:6**).

 The color of the pixels that are added when you increase the canvas size is determined by the background color of the Photoshop color-picker. The default color is white. For more on the color-picker, see FIGURE 9:32, *Choosing Color*.

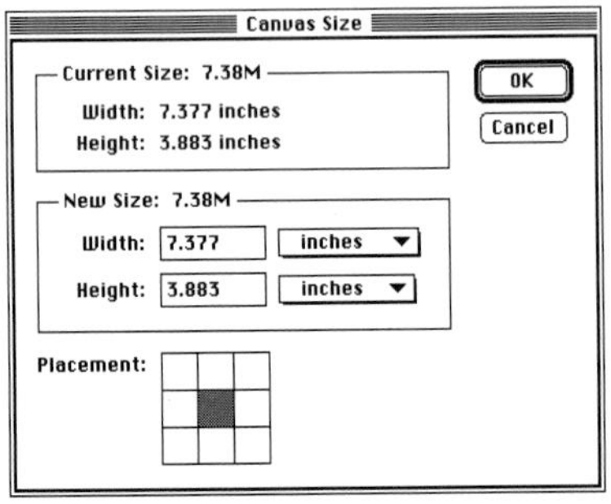

The Canvas Size dialog box lets you add extra space to the work area of an image.

FIGURE 4:6

To change an image's resolution without affecting its width or height, open the Image Size dialog box under the Image menu. Uncheck the File Size box and enter the desired number of pixels per inch in the Resolution box.

FIGURE A was scanned at 400 ppi. FIGURE B has been resampled (pixels added or subtracted) down to 200 ppi. Note that there has been little change in image quality, but the file size has changed significantly—from 3.26 MB to 835 K. Often pictures have too much resolution. If you are making four-color separations, there are not many instances in which 400 ppi is necessary (see FIGURE 4:3, *Comparing Image Resolutions*) so you should sample the scan down. The resulting dramatic decrease in file size will be important when you work with artwork that is larger and in color.

FIGURE C has been resampled down even further to 60 ppi, and now there is a very noticeable change in image quality. Resolution can be increased but this practice should be avoided. Photoshop must guess how to add pixels to a picture when you increase resolution, which results in an apparently out-of-focus image. If you need more pixels per inch, rescan at a higher resolution. FIGURE D has been resampled up to 200 ppi from 60 ppi, and the results are not good; if anything, D looks worse than C.

© 1994 ROB DAY, FROM A COMPOSITE OF THIRTEEN 35MM NEGATIVES SCANNED WITH A NIKON LS-3500 SCANNER, AND ASSEMBLED WITH PHOTOSHOP

SCANNING

5

Desktop scanners have a reputation for being useless for anything other
than creating for-position-only art. While
the raw scans of most desktop scanners
are too crude for commercially acceptable work, most can be greatly improved
with Photoshop. Because desktop scans
need to be color-corrected, sharpened,
and converted to CMYK, they are not very
valuable in a production setting where
the aim is to reproduce an original as
quickly as possible. However, for artistic
uses, the spontaneity of having a scanner
always available is usually worth the extra
time spent making corrections. The quality of the final output will depend on how
skillfully you adjust the raw scan. This
chapter and the next two, *Color Correction* and *Sharpening,* cover techniques
for making a desktop scan commercially
acceptable.

THE SCANNER'S SOFTWARE

Your scanner comes with software that drives the scanner (**FIGURE 5:1**). The software can be either a stand-alone application, or a Photoshop plug-in. The plug-in is more convenient in that you make the scan from within Photoshop. After making the scan, it is automatically opened into Photoshop as an untitled document. You can then work on the scan before deciding whether it should be saved.

 If you do not have a plug-in for your scanner, call the manufacturer to see if one is available. If you have the scanner plug-in, it should appear as an item in the Acquire submenu under the File menu. If it does not show up under Acquire, make sure that the scanner plug-in resides in the folder that has been designated as the Plug-ins folder in the Plug-ins submenu under Preferences (**FIGURE 5:2**).

The scanner software allows you to adjust the way the scan will be made—its resolution, output dimensions, brightness, contrast, and color balance. In most cases these adjustments are made via the scanner's software, not by an adjustment in the hardware. This is an important concept to understand, because in most cases the results will be better if these operations are performed after the scanning with Photoshop, rather than with the scanner's software.

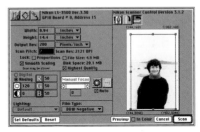

FIGURE 5:1

Your scanner comes with software that drives the scanner. Here are the scanner software interfaces for a flatbed (Microtek) and slide (Nikon) scanner.

FIGURE 5:2

Most scanners have a Photoshop plug-in available that lets you access the scanner's software from within Photoshop via the Acquire submenu under File. The scanner's plug-in should be copied into the Photoshop Plug-ins folder.

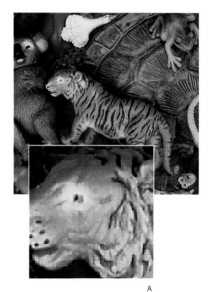

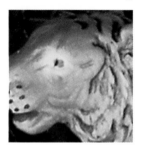

A

FIGURE 5:3   B

SCANNER RESOLUTION   Most scanners have one optical or native resolution. It is important to know the optical resolution of your scanner, because usually the scan will be of higher quality if you make the initial scan at the optical resolution, and then resample it with Photoshop. For example, my flatbed scanner's optical resolution is 300 ppi, so I always scan at 300 ppi and 100%, and then resample or resize the file if necessary with Photoshop. I do have the option in the scanner interface to adjust the resolution, but the scanner software resamples the image on the fly and artifacts start to show (**FIGURE 5:3**).

Many scanners are advertised as having a higher resolution than their actual optical resolution. This higher resolution is accomplished via software, which is undesirable for grayscale and color work (see FIGURE 4:5, *Changing Image Resolutions*). However, line art can benefit from interpolation; see FIGURE 5:4, *Scanning Line Art*.

SCANNER TONAL CORRECTIONS   You can also adjust the brightness, contrast, and color of the scan using the scanner's software. As is the case with resolution, usually it is best to leave the scanner's software at its defaults and then adjust the file with Photoshop. The default settings will usually provide a starting scan with the highest levels of gray.

Each time you adjust the tonality of an image via software, parts of the grayscale are lost. The amount of lost gray values depends on how radically you adjust the image (if you are working in color, the loss can occur in any of the three RGB channels). For example, you might start with an image that has a full grayscale (256 levels of gray) and slightly adjust its contrast. After this adjustment there might be only 250 levels of gray. Because printing presses are not

Scanning Line Art

Black and white line art (Bitmap Mode) usually needs more resolution—between 800 and 1200 ppi—than grayscale or color
art. If your scanner's resolution is only 300 ppi, you can use the
following method to improve the appearance of line art:

1 Scan the art at 100% and 300 ppi as a grayscale (FIGURE A).

2 Size the scan to its output dimensions and increase its resolution to 1,000 ppi. Make sure that Interpolation is set at
Bicubic in the Preferences file. The file size will become ten
times larger and the edges of the line art will be blurred
(FIGURE B).

3 Choose Levels and move the left and right Input sliders to
the center to sharpen the edges of the line art (FIGURE C).
Click OK.

4 Choose Bitmap from the Mode menu. Leave the Input and
Output resolution at 1,000 pixels/inch and choose Diffusion Dither as the Conversion Method. You can also choose
50% Threshold, but I find that Diffusion Dither makes a
smoother transition along a line's edges. The bitmap's file
size is now an eighth that of the grayscale, and the line art
will print from an imagesetter at 1,000 dpi. Because your
monitor can display only 72 ppi, the art will preview with
jagged edges, but it will print smoothly (FIGURE D).

A

B

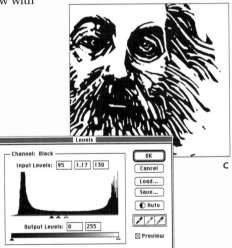

C

D

Each time you adjust the grayscale of an image, gray values can be lost. The Levels graph in figure A is from a scan made at the scanner's default setting. Figure B shows the Levels graph after adjusting the brightness and contrast in the scanner's software then rescanning. Scanning at the defaults and then making adjustments with Photoshop in as few moves as possible ensures the fullest grayscale for output.

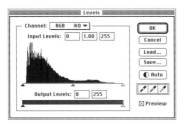

A

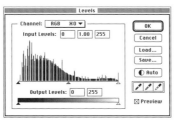

FIGURE 5:5   B

capable of printing 256 distinguishable levels of gray, the loss of 5 miscellaneous gray levels would not be noticeable when the image is printed (unless all 5 values occur at the same spot on the grayscale). However, radical adjustments in contrast—or multiple adjustments—would drop more gray levels, to the point where it might be noticeable on press. It is best to start with a scan that has as many gray levels per channel as possible.

It is easy to determine if your scanner's settings adjust an image via software. Make a scan at the default settings and then rescan after adjusting the brightness and contrast settings in the scanner's interface. Click on the window of the first scan and choose Levels from the Image menu. The Levels dialog box shows a graph of the picture's gray values plotted from black on the left, to white on the right. Each vertical spike represents the number of pixels at that gray level.

As you can see, the graph of a scan made at the default settings from my flatbed scanner has very few gaps in the grayscale. The scan made after adjusting the brightness and contrast with the scanner's interface yields a graph that covers more of the grayscale but has gaps, which indicates the adjustments are being made via software rather than hardware (**FIGURE 5:5**).

Some mid- to expensive-range scanners scan at more than 8 bits (or 256 gray levels) per channel and interpolate the best 256 gray levels from the extra data. In this case it might be an advantage to adjust the image with the scanner's software in order to get the best grayscale.

MAKING AN ACCURATE SCAN

Another reason for using the scanner's default settings is that it can be very difficult to see the thumbnail-sized preview provided by most scanner softwares. If you are not worried about making resolution and tonal adjustments, you can simply use the preview as a means of making a rough crop, and then make the final crop in Photoshop where the image can be clearly seen. Below is the sequence I use for making an accurate scan:

1 Choose your scanner's plug-in from the Acquire submenu under File (**FIGURE 5:6**).

2 Set the scaling to 100%, and the resolution to your scanner's optical resolution (**FIGURE 5:7**).

3 Choose Prescan to make a preview, roughly crop the image, and click Scan (**FIGURE 5:8**).

4 When the scan is finished, double-click the Hand tool and the scan's entire preview will automatically fit, as largely as is possible, within your monitor's display area (**FIGURE 5:9**).

5 Double-click the Crop tool and the Crop Tool Options palette is opened. Make sure that the

If your scanner's Photoshop plug-in is placed in the active Plug-ins folder, it will appear in the Acquire submenu under File.

FIGURE 5:6

Your scanner's software should be set at its optical resolution and 100% scaling for the best initial scan.

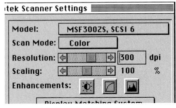

FIGURE 5:7

Most scanner's have a very small preview, so set the scanner's crop tool loosely around the image and make the final crop with Photoshop.

FIGURE 5:8

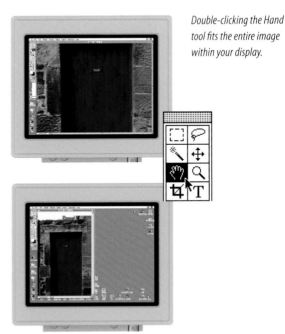

Double-clicking the Hand tool fits the entire image within your display.

FIGURE 5:9

Fixed Target Size box is checked. Enter the dimensions at which you want the image to print in the Width and Height boxes and leave the Resolution box blank (**FIGURE 5:10**).

6 Click and drag inside the scan's window and the Crop marquee appears. Adjust the Crop marquee by clicking and dragging on its corner points. The marquee will be constrained to the proportions of the dimensions you entered in the Options palette. You can also enter one dimension—in this case the crop marquee will not be proportionally constrained. Holding

down the Option key and clicking and dragging on one of the corner points rotates the marquee (**FIGURE 5:11**). When you have adjusted the marquee, move the cursor inside of the marquee and it will become a scissors icon. Click once and the image is cropped to the dimensions you specified (**FIGURE 5:12**).

Because you did not enter a number in the Resolution box of the Crop Tool Options palette, the resolution of your cropped scan is proportionally constrained to the width and height you specified—the pixels are resized, not resampled. The resolution of the image is now the highest it can be at the specified dimensions, while scanning at your scanner's optical resolution. In many cases the resulting resolution is too high and the image should be sampled down. For more on the Crop Tool Options, see **FIGURE 5:13**, *The Crop Tool*.

Enter the maximum dimensions that the image will print at in the Width and Height boxes of the Crop Tool Options palette. Leave the Resolution box blank.

FIGURE 5:10

You can rotate the Crop tool's marquee by pressing the Option key and clicking and dragging on the marquee's corner points.

FIGURE 5:11

FIGURE 5:12

Moving your cursor inside the marquee turns it to a scissors icon clicking once crops the picture.

The Crop Tool

The Crop tool can be used for much more than cropping away part of a picture:

- Double-clicking the Crop tool opens the Crop Tool Options palette. Checking Fixed Target Size lets you specify output dimensions and resolution for the crop (FIGURE A). If you enter a dimension in both the Width and Height boxes, but not the Resolution box, the image will be resized to those dimensions when you make the crop.

- If you also enter a number in the Resolution box, the image will be resized and resampled to the dimensions and resolution specified. When specifying resolution in the Crop Tool Options palette, use caution that you do not upsample the image—when in doubt leave the Resolution box blank and, if necessary, resample via Image Size later.

- If you hold down the Option key and click and drag on a crop marquee's corner points, the marquee can be rotated. You can also move the marquee without changing its size by holding down the Command key, then clicking and dragging on a corner point (FIGURE 5:11).

- You can quickly match the dimensions and resolution of another image by opening the image you want to match, and clicking Front Image in Crop Tool Options. The dimensions and resolution of the active Photoshop window are automatically entered in the Crop Tool Options palette. Any images that you crop will be resized to these dimensions and resolution (FIGURE B).

- You can size all of your images to fit a specific column width when you export them to a page layout program. Choose Units from the Preferences submenu under File. Enter the dimensions of your page's column and gutter in the Column Size Width and Gutter boxes—you can specify the units of measure by clicking on the pop-up menus next to Width and Gutter. Click OK. In the Crop Tool Options palette choose columns from the pop-up menu next to the Width box. Enter the number of columns you want the picture to fit into and any subsequent crops you make will automatically fit the image to the specified number of columns.

- Unchecking the Fixed Target Size box removes any constraints from the Crop tool.

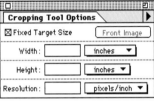

A

B

To specify the final image resolution, choose Image Size from the Image menu. In some cases the image resolution might be lower than the desired output resolution (see FIGURE 4:2, *The 2:1 Ratio*). If the resolution is too low, the scan should be made on another scanner with a higher optical resolution. Uncheck File Size and enter the desired resolution (see FIGURE 4:5, *Changing Image Resolution*). Click OK and the image is resampled and its file size is adjusted accordingly (FIGURE 5:14).

 If you intend to export the image to another program where it might be resized, make sure the dimensions you specify in Photoshop are large enough so that the image will always be sized down in the layout program.

CALCULATING FILE SIZES   You may find that it is useful to know what the file size of an image will be before starting to scan. You can quickly determine file size by using the New dialog box as a file size calculator. Choose New from the File menu. A dialog box appears (FIGURE 5:15). Click next to Mode and choose the desired color mode from the pop-up menu—Bitmap, Grayscale, RGB, CMYK, or Lab Color. There are also pop-up menus that allow you to choose the Width, Height, and Resolution measurement units. Type in the desired width, height, and resolution, and Image Size will change accordingly. Note the file size and click Cancel.

The resampled file is now the correct resolution and dimensions.

FIGURE 5:14

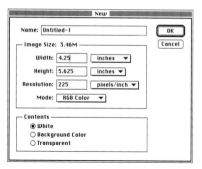

FIGURE 5:15

The New dialog box can be used as a file size calculator. Entering the image dimensions and resolution, and changing the Mode, causes the Image Size to change accordingly.

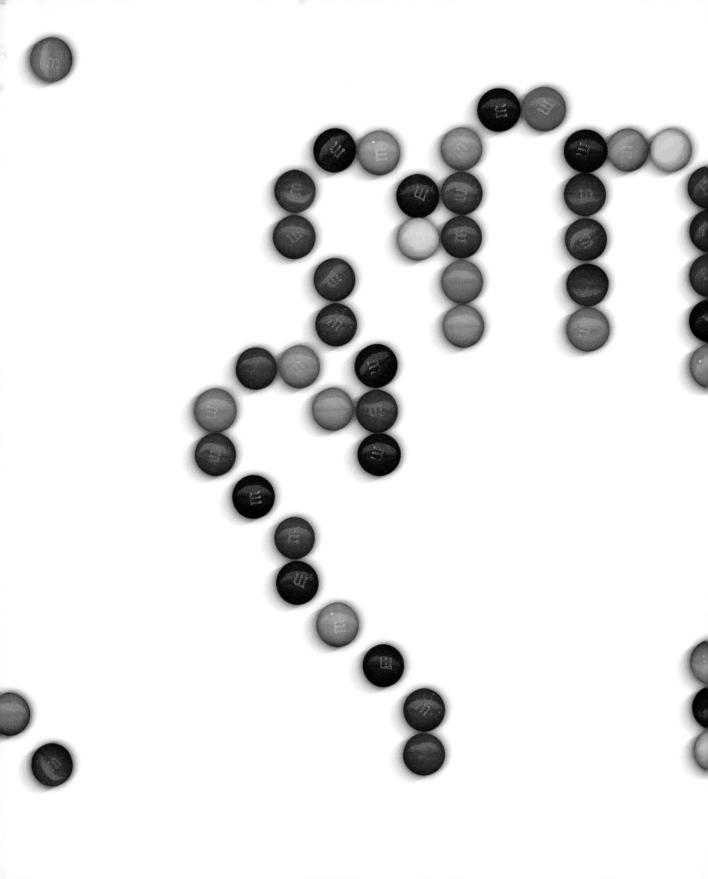

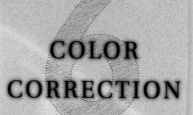

COLOR CORRECTION

ONCE YOU HAVE MADE THE INITIAL scan, you can use Photoshop to adjust tonality and color either globally or to specific areas of the image. This chapter will cover how to use Photoshop's image adjustment tools. Keep in mind that if you are going to make adjustments based on what you see on your monitor, you should set your monitor to the proper color temperature and gamma. Also, you should work under stable ambient light conditions before making any color corrections to an image (see Chapter Two, *Working Conditions*). You should also read Chapter Fifteen, *Color Management*, before attempting to print an important project.

ADJUSTING A GRAYSCALE IMAGE

The tools for adjusting an image's grayscale and color are found under the Adjust submenu under Image. The first three—Levels, Curves, and Brightness/Contrast, are the most commonly used adjustment tools. You can use them for adjusting either a grayscale or color image. Starting with grayscale is an easy way to learn these three tools.

BRIGHTNESS / CONTRAST   The easiest, but least sophisticated, way to adjust value is with Brightness/Contrast. The dialog box is self-explanatory—moving the top slider right or left lightens or darkens the image. Moving the bottom slider increases or decreases contrast (**FIGURE 6:1**).

LEVELS   Levels is less straightforward, but has more options than Brightness/Contrast. The Levels dialog box (Command+L) shows a graph labeled Input Levels with three small adjustment triangles beneath its baseline, and below that a grayscale bar labeled Output Levels with two small adjustment triangles (**FIGURE 6:2**).

The Input Levels graph is also called a histogram. It is a representation of the 256 possible gray levels, from 0 on the left representing pure black, to 255 on the right representing pure white. Each vertical black line represents the number of pixels in the image or selection at a given level along the grayscale. Images with good contrast will show a Levels graph with vertical lines that are spread across most of the scale from white to black. Conversely, an image with low contrast will show a graph with the vertical lines clumped in one spot.

FIGURE 6:3 shows the Levels dialog box for a scan made on my Microtek 300z flatbed scanner using the

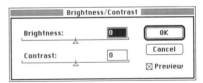
FIGURE 6:1

Brightness/Contrast is the simplest yet most limited of the adjustment tools.

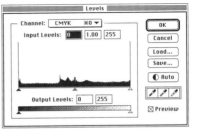
FIGURE 6:2

Levels lets you adjust the midtones of a picture.

FIGURE 6:3

The Levels histogram for this raw scan shows that most of the values are grouped at the dark end of the grayscale. Adjusting the middle triangle of the input scale to the left brightens the image and redistributes the histogram.

If an image lacks contrast there will be no values at the ends of the scale. Moving the left-hand black triangle to the right and the white right-hand triangle to the left will add contrast to the image and the resulting histogram will cover more of the grayscale.

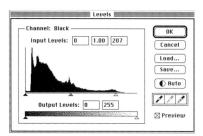

FIGURE 6:4

Clicking the Auto button in Levels automatically redistributes the image's values across the entire grayscale. However, using Auto is not necessarily the best move, as it can cause the image to become overly contrasted.

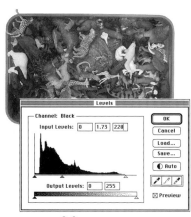

FIGURE 6:5

Moving the white point slider not as far to the left results in an image where all the highlights have at least some percentage of halftone dot.

FIGURE 6:6

default settings. The graph shows that most of the values of the scan are grouped between the left and the middle of the graph, resulting in a printed image that is overly dark. If you click and drag on any of the small triangles in Levels, the grayscale of the image changes interactively. When you click OK, the changes are applied to the currently selected area or, if nothing is selected, to the entire image.

The middle triangle beneath the Input Levels graph adjusts the mid-tones of an image without significantly affecting the highlights or shadows. Photographers refer to this mid-tone change as *gamma adjustment*. Sliding the middle triangle to the left lightens the image; sliding it to the right darkens the image. Sliding the white triangle on the right to the left brightens the highlights; moving the black triangle on the left to the right darkens the shadows. Both of these moves increase the contrast of the image.

If the Level's Histogram does not span the entire grayscale, you can move the white and black triangles inward until they touch the first pixels on each side of the scale (**FIGURE 6:4**). Clicking OK after this move will distribute the gray levels evenly from black to white (clicking on the Auto button in the Levels dialog box accomplishes the same thing automatically). Automatically adjusting the image this way is not necessarily a good thing since most images should not have pure whites and blacks. You can see from **FIGURE 6:5** that clicking the auto button for this scan makes the resulting print overly contrasted. A better move is to brighten the image by moving the middle slider to the left and the white point slider just slightly to the left (**FIGURE 6:6**). This ensures that there will be at least some values in the highlights.

If you adjust the two triangles under the Output Levels grayscale bar, the image loses contrast. Moving the white triangle on the right darkens the highlights, and moving the black triangle on the left lightens the shadows. **FIGURE 6:7** shows how moving the black Output slider to the right lightens the shadows. Adjusting these five triangles gives you much more control over the image's values than you have using the Brightness/Contrast tool.

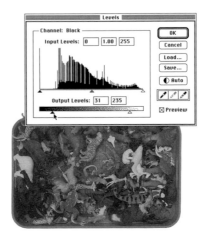

Moving the two output sliders inward lightens the shadows and darkens the highlights, which lowers contrast.

 The Levels dialog box and all of the other adjustment dialogs have a Preview checkbox. If the Preview box is checked, the changes you make do not happen interactively until you release the mouse button. When you do release the mouse button only the current selection is updated with the new change; the nonselected portions of the image remain unchanged. If the Preview box is left unchecked, then the changes occur interactively, but to the entire screen.

FIGURE 6:7

CURVES Curves gives you the most control adjusting an image's values. The Curves dialog box is modeled after the controls for adjusting color and value on traditional electronic pre-press systems. The dialog box (Command + M) shows a graph that plots the Input levels (the values, from 0% to 100%, in the picture as they currently exist) on the horizontal x axis against the Output levels (the new values as you adjust the curve) on the vertical y axis (**FIGURE 6:8**).

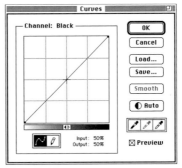

The Curves dialog box lets you adjust the grayscale along a curve and gives you the most control over an image.

FIGURE 6:8

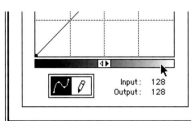

FIGURE 6:9

Clicking on the grayscale bar under the Curves graph toggles the input/output readout from gray values (256 to 0) to percentages (0 to 100). It also reverses the curve.

 You can choose whether you want to have the Curve's Input levels to read as white on the right and black on the left, or vice versa. Clicking on the grayscale bar under the graph toggles between the two modes (**FIGURE 6:9**). When white is on the left, the readout is as percentages from 0 to 100. When white is on the right, the readout is in gray levels from 256 to 0. Here I am working with white on the left.

When you open the Curves dialog box, the line on the graph is diagonal because the Input and Output values are the same. Clicking on the diagonal line plots a point that can be adjusted. For instance, if you click on the center of the diagonal line, Input and Output both read 50%. By pulling the point straight down, the Output readout changes to a smaller percentage while Input remains the same. This means that the 50% middle gray will be lightened to the new Output percentage. The image's other values will also be lightened, but on a gradual curve until there is no change at the 0 and 100% levels (**FIGURE 6:10**). This curve increases contrast as the image is lightened or darkened.

If you choose Show Info from the Palettes submenu under the Window menu, the Info palette appears (see **FIGURE 6:11**, *The Info Palette*). With the Info palette visible, and the Curves dialog open, the Info readout will show two numbers when you move the cursor into the image area. The number on the left indicates the values as they were before adjusting

Clicking on the center of the curve and dragging down brightens the mid-tone.

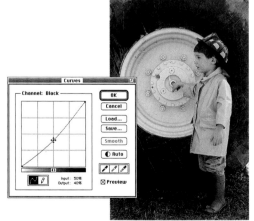

FIGURE 6:10

the curve; the number on the right indicates the values that will result from the adjustment (**FIGURE 6:12**). This feature also exists for the other image adjustment tools.

 If you are applying the same curve to many documents Option+Command+M opens Curves with the last curve applied loaded. Also, Photoshop 3.0's Curves dialog box has a zoom box in the upper right-hand corner which expands the size of the dialog.

Plotting multiple points along the curve allows control over different portions of the image's grayscale. For example, if you want to affect an image's quarter-tones, plot a point on the diagonal's center mark so that

FIGURE 6:11

The Info Palette

The Info palette is very useful when you are adjusting an image's color and values. Click on the arrow in the palette's upper righthand corner to access the Info Options dialog box. You can choose to show either one or two color-mode readouts by checking or unchecking the Show First Color Readout or Show Second Color Readout check boxes (FIGURE A). Clicking on the Mode pop-up menu lets you choose the color mode that the readout's values will be displayed as—choosing the same color mode in both readouts results in the Info palette showing only one readout.

The most useful combination is Actual Color as the first readout, and CMYK Color as the second readout. With Actual Color chosen as the first readout, the first set of values are based on the image's current mode. With CMYK Color chosen as the second readout, the second set of values show how the current mode's values would convert to CMYK, based on your Monitor, Printing Inks, and Separation Setups (see Chapter Fifteen, *Color Management*). You can also bypass the Info Options dialog box by clicking and dragging on the eyedropper icons in the Info palette to access the mode pop-up menu (FIGURE B).

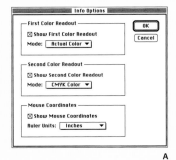

A

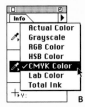

B

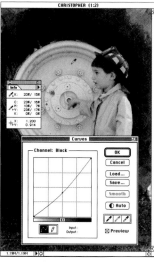

Showing the Info palette lets you view the image's values as they were before making a move, and as they are as a result of the curve when it is applied.

FIGURE 6:12

the readout is Input: 50% and Output: 50%, then plot another point at Input: 25% and move the 25% point up or down. This will darken or lighten the quarter-tones, while the mid-tones stay anchored.

Notice that when the cursor is outside of the dialog box and on the active window it becomes an eye-dropper. Clicking on the image with the eyedropper creates a circle on the curve that relates to the pixel that has been clicked on. If you want to lighten or darken a specific gray level of an image, click on it with the eyedropper and note where the circle appears on the curve. Then plot a point there and move it up to darken, or down to lighten that part of the grayscale (**FIGURE 6:13**). If you are working in CMYK mode, the eyedropper works only when Cyan, Magenta, Yellow, or Black are chosen from the Channel pop-up menu.

Moving the cursor outside the Curves dialog box changes it to an Eyedropper cursor. Clicking causes a circle to appear on the curve that corresponds to the value of the pixel under the tip of the eyedropper. This tool is useful for choosing specific gray levels of the image that you want to adjust. In this case, the gray level I will adjust is 27%.

By plotting a point at the 50% and 75% marks of the graph, I have anchored the mid- and three-quarter tones, allowing me to brighten the quarter tones independent from the other tones. Here I have changed the 27% values to 18%.

FIGURE 6:13

You can adjust the way the Eyedropper cursor reads the pixel information by double-clicking on the Eyedropper tool and choosing either Point Sample, 3 by 3 Average, or 5 by 5 Average from the Eyedropper Options palette (**FIGURE 6:14**). Choosing 3 by 3 or 5 by 5 Average prevents you from choosing a random pixel value that is not representative of the values in the area you click on.

ADJUSTING A COLOR IMAGE

Brightness/Contrast, Levels, and Curves can also be used to adjust color images. Plus, there are five additional tools that can be used to adjust color in a variety of ways. Color Balance, Hue/Saturation, Replace Color, Selective Color, and Variations allow you to solve just about any color correction problem. Replace Color and Selective Color are new features to Photoshop 3.0 and they make it easier to adjust specific parts of an image without first making complex selections.

COLOR CORRECTING WITH LEVELS AND CURVES Both the Levels and Curves tools also allow you to adjust the tonality of a color image. If you are in a color mode (RGB, CMYK, or Lab) you can adjust the overall brightness and contrast of an image, or you can adjust the individual channels, which allows you to change the color balance of the picture (**FIGURE 6:15**).

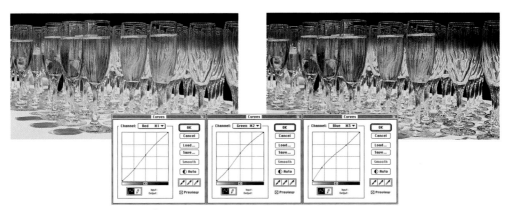

FIGURE 6:15

The Eyedropper Tool Options lets you adjust how a value is read. Point Sample samples one pixel at a time, while 3 by 3 and 5 by 5 Average shows the value as an average of 9 or 25 pixels around the point of the eyedropper.

FIGURE 6:14

You can adjust an image's color balance by choosing one of its channels from the Levels or Curves Channel pop-up menu and then adjusting the channel.

You can adjust two of the channels at once by shift-clicking on the desired channels in the Channels palette.

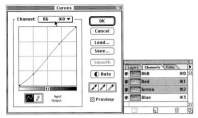

FIGURE 6:16

 Depending on its mode, a color picture always has three (RGB or Lab) or four (CMYK) grayscale channels that are combined to make the color image. For more on color modes see Chapter Fifteen, *Color Management*.

To adjust a single color channel, open Levels or Curves and click on the pop-up menu next to Channel and select the channel you want to adjust. If you are in Levels, the Histogram will reflect the values of that channel. Make your correction and click OK. You can also adjust any combination of channels via the Channels palette. Choose Show Channels from the Palettes submenu to access the Channels palette. Shift-click the channels you want to correct, and click the eye next to the composite channel to show the full color preview. Open Levels or Curves and any adjustment will be made only to the selected channels (**FIGURE 6:16**). For more on the Channels palette see Chapter Ten, *Masks and Channels.*

Color Balance lets you adjust the overall color cast of an image. Clicking on the Preserve Luminance box maintains the contrast of the image as the color is shifted.

FIGURE 6:17

COLOR BALANCE   Choosing Color Balance from the Adjust submenu under the Image menu (Command+Y) opens the Color Balance dialog box, which allows you to adjust the picture's color balance. This tool lets you remove overall color-casts from a picture. The dialog box shows three horizontal lines with cyan, magenta, and yellow on the left, and red, green, and blue on the right; moving the center triangles adjusts the color of the current selection. You can also choose to affect the shadows, midtones, or highlights by clicking the radio buttons at the bottom of the dialog box. If you check the Preserve Luminance box, then the overall brightness and contrast of the image will be preserved while color is added or subtracted (**FIGURE 6:17**).

HUE / SATURATION Hue/Saturation (Command + H) allows you to make more specific color corrections to an image than the Color Correction dialog box does. The dialog box has three sliders labeled Hue, Saturation, and Lightness. Moving the Hue slider to the right changes the hue of the pixels clockwise around the color wheel (**FIGURE 6:18**). Moving the Saturation slider to the left desaturates the pixels, and moving the Lightness slider to the left darkens the image. There are also radio buttons for the RGB/CMY colors at the left of the dialog box. Clicking on one of these buttons allows you to adjust the Hue, Saturation, and Lightness of specific hues within the image. For example, you can lighten and add yellow to all of the reds in a picture by clicking the R radio button and moving the Hue and Lightness slider to the right (**FIGURE 6:19**).

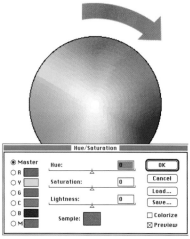

Moving the Hue slider to the right moves the pixels' hue clockwise around the color wheel.

FIGURE 6:18

 When you lighten an image using the Lightness slider in Hue/Saturation, the pixels are uniformly lightened or darkened—the image is not adjusted on a curve. In this case the image will lose contrast as it is lightened or darkened.

REPLACE COLOR Photoshop 3.0 adds two new color-correcting tools to the Adjust submenu—Replace Color and Selective Color. Replace Color is a very powerful color correcting tool as it lets you adjust specific parts of a picture without first making a selection (see **FIGURE 9:13**).

The Replace Color dialog box shows a grayscale mask (when the Selection radio button is clicked on) that is created by clicking on the picture you are adjusting. The pixel that you click on is the starting point for the mask. White areas of the mask represent the portion of the picture that will be most affected by color adjustments, and the black areas are protected from any changes. Moving the Fuzziness slider

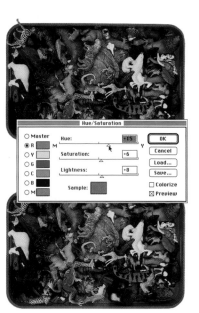

Clicking on the R, G, B, C, M, or Y radio buttons lets you adjust specific colors within an image.

FIGURE 6:19

The Replace Color dialog box shows a black and white preview of a mask that represents areas of the image that can be adjusted with white. Moving the Fuzziness slider expands or contracts the mask.

FIGURE 6:20

to the right expands the white, or open, areas of the mask, based on the value of the pixel you have clicked on (**FIGURE 6:20**).

You can also expand the open areas of the mask further, by clicking on the eyedropper icon with the plus sign, and clicking on the image again (holding down the shift key is a shortcut for accessing the Eyedropper+ tool). For example, you could first click on a specific light blue area of the image, and then with the eyedropper/plus selected, click on the shadows of the blue area to expand the selection (**FIGURE 6:21**). When you have finished adjusting the mask, then adjusting the Hue, Saturation, Lightness sliders affects only the part of the image represented by the mask's white areas (**FIGURE 6:22**). Click the Image radio button to preview the original image in the dialog box, and compare it to the adjusted image.

Clicking on the eyedropper+ icon lets you add other pixel colors to the mask each time you click on the image. Here I have added both red and green pixels to the mask.

FIGURE 6:21

Once you are satisfied with the mask you can adjust the Hue, Saturation, and Lightness of the areas of the image represented by the white areas of the mask.

FIGURE 6:22

SELECTIVE COLOR   Once you have converted a file from RGB to CMYK, it is often necessary to fine-tune delicate areas such as highlights, neutral grays, and shadows. When you open the Selective Color dialog box, clicking on the Colors pop-up menu lets you choose Whites, Neutrals, Blacks, and any of the C, M, Y, R, G, or B colors (**FIGURE 6:23**). You can also choose Relative or Absolute as the Method. With Relative checked, the adjustments you make to the image are based on a percentage relative to the existing values. If you choose Absolute as the Method, an absolute percentage is added to the values—the percentage added is more or less dependent on how close the pixel colors are to the color chosen in the Color pop-up menu. The Absolute method will add or subtract more color from the image than the Relative method.

Selective Color allows you to fine-tune the CMYK values of the finished picture, ensuring that the highlights and neutral areas don't have any unwanted color casts. For example, if the picture's highlights were made of 12% cyan, 5% magenta, and 13% yellow, they would have a green cast. With Selective Color you could choose Whites as the Color, Absolute as the Method, and move the Cyan slider to –13% which would give a new highlight of 3% cyan, 5% magenta, 13% yellow (**FIGURE 6:24**).

 You can use Selective Color in any color mode. If you use it in RGB Mode, then the Monitor, Printing Inks, and Separation Setups found under the Preferences submenu determine which CMYK values are assigned to the RGB colors (see Chapter Fifteen, *Color Management*).

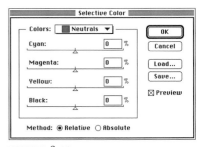

FIGURE 6:23

The Selective Color dialog box lets you choose Whites, Blacks, Neutrals or any of the primary colors for adjustment.

You can fine-tune the CMYK values of an image's highlights by choosing Whites from the Colors pop-up menu.

FIGURE 6:24

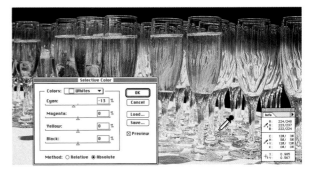

Variations provides an intuitive interface for adjusting an image's color.

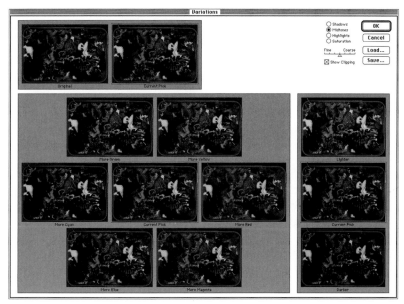

FIGURE 6:25

VARIATIONS   If the above color-correction tools seem less than intuitive, then Variations provides a more visual approach to adjusting color. When you choose Variations, the Variations dialog box appears. The upper left corner shows two thumbnail versions of the image—the original image and the image as you make changes. The center of the dialog shows the image surrounded by six versions of the image that have more of the six primary colors added to them. Clicking and dragging one of these into the center image adjusts the Current Pick's color. You can also lighten or darken the image by dragging and dropping the versions labeled Lighter or Darker. If you check the Show Clipping box, an overlay will show in the preview box that indicates any areas of the image that are pure black or white. The small size of the Variations previews can make subtle corrections difficult (**FIGURE 6:25**).

SHARPENING
7

Aｌｌ ｓｃａｎｓ ｎｅｅｄ ｓｏｍｅ ｄｅｇｒｅｅ ｏｆ sharpening applied to them. Desktop scanners usually provide no means of sharpening a scan in their software, or if they do the controls are limited. High-end scanners allow the operator to specify the scan's sharpness, and the sharpening is done via the scanner's software. Without sharpening, a scan will have a soft appearance on output. This softness can give the image the appearance of not having enough resolution, even though its resolution is adequate.

Photoshop has a number of filters that can be used to sharpen a desktop scan. Sharpen, Sharpen More, and Sharpen Edges are generic filters that you apply to the image without any controls, so their uses are limited (FIGURE 7:1). The Unsharp Mask filter, despite its misleading name, gives you the most control over how an image is sharpened, and that is the filter I will be demonstrating here. How you sharpen a scan with Unsharp Mask depends on a number of factors: the image resolution, grain of the photograph, the halftone screen, and your personal taste all come into play.

THE UNSHARP MASK FILTER

The Unsharp Mask filter is found in the Sharpen submenu under the Filter menu. The dialog box contains a small preview of the image and three sliders labeled Amount, Radius, and Threshold. If you move your cursor onto the image it turns to a small square. Clicking on the image determines which part of the image is previewed in the dialog box. The ratio beneath the preview indicates the preview's magnification—click + or – to zoom in or out (FIGURE 7:2).

AMOUNT   The amount slider lets you adjust the intensity of the sharpening. Amount is measured in percentage from 0% to 500%. The apparent intensity of the sharpening results from the combination of Amount, Radius, and Threshold. Radius increases the sharpening along the image's edges, while Threshold softens the sharpening in smooth areas of the picture.

 Because the preview of a correctly sharpened image at a less than 1:1 monitor-to-image ratio can appear distorted, sharpening should be one of the final operations you perform (see FIGURE 7:3, *Previewing a Sharpened Image*).

A   B

FIGURE 7:1   C   D

Sharpen (B), Sharpen More (C), and Sharpen Edges (D) are generic sharpening filters which provide no controls. Figure A is not sharpened.

FIGURE 7:2

After opening the Unsharp Mask dialog box, your cursor becomes a small square when you move it onto the image. Clicking on the image previews that part of the image in the dialog box.

Previewing a Sharpened Image

Because your monitor's pixel resolution is relatively low it can be difficult to get an accurate view of how a sharpened image will look on the printed page. An image with a correct amount of Unsharp Masking applied can look terrible when previewed at monitor to image ratios of less than 1:1 (FIGURE A), but look correct when it is printed (FIGURE B). You should judge the sharpened image at a ratio of 1:1, but even then the sharpening will look slightly exaggerated, as you are viewing the picture dimensionally larger than it will print on the page (FIGURE C).

A

B

C

RADIUS   Most of the sharpening in an image occurs along the edges of the image detail—for example, the twigs of a tree against a light sky. The Radius setting lets you adjust the number of pixels that are adjusted on each side of the edges. The Radius can be set from 0.1 to 250 pixels.

Using a Radius value that is too high can result in keylining. Keylining is an unwanted artifact at the edges that looks like a dark outline (**FIGURE 7:4**). If the Radius setting is too low, then the grain of the original photograph can be exaggerated.

THRESHOLD   Most scanners add a certain amount of noise to the image in the scanning process. The combination of noise and photographic grain can make an image appear overly grainy if it is sharpened incorrectly. The Threshold setting lets you determine the range of values, from 0 to 255, that determine an edge. Increasing the Threshold setting softens the effect of sharpening in areas of the image that are smooth, and where increasing the appearance of noise is undesirable (**FIGURE 7:5**).

Using a Radius setting that is too high can result in keylining.

FIGURE 7:4

Increasing the Threshold setting can help prevent unwanted noise.

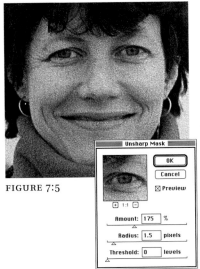

FIGURE 7:5

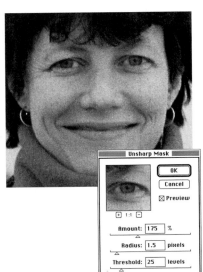

CHOOSING AN UNSHARP MASK SETTING

The Unsharp mask settings that you choose depend largely on the type of image, its resolution, and the halftone screen. Because all these factors are important, there is no single correct way to sharpen scans. An image that is not sharpened enough can appear not to have enough resolution, and if a scan is overly sharpened unwanted artifacts might show in the printed piece. Following are some guidelines for applying the Unsharp Mask filter in a variety of situations

UNSHARP MASKING AND IMAGE RESOLUTION   How much effect the Amount and Radius settings have on the sharpening of the scan is influenced by the image's resolution. Scans with high resolution need a larger Radius setting than scans with low resolution in order for the sharpening to have a similar appearance in both cases. **FIGURE 7:6** shows three images at varying resolutions with the same Amount and Radius applied. As you can see, the sharpening is more exaggerated in the low-resolution image even though the same amounts have been applied.

FIGURE 7:6   *150 ppi*   *300 ppi*   *600 ppi*

Sharpening is dependent on resolution, so images with different resolutions need different amounts of sharpening. Here is the same image at three different image resolutions, with the same unsharp masking applied.

AVOIDING UNWANTED NOISE AND KEYLINES

Incorrect sharpening often will result in artifacts. The artifacts usually show as unwanted noise, or as keylines—a distinctive outline along the image's contours. The amount of noise in the starting scan depends mostly on the quality of the photograph. A photograph shot with slow-speed film (50 to 200 ISO) has much less grain than a photograph shot with high-speed film (400 to 1,600 ISO). If the starting photograph is very grainy, then the sharpening process can exaggerate the grain. In this case a lower Amount, and higher Radius and Threshold, will sharpen the image's edges without accentuating the grain. You have to be careful though; increasing the Radius too much will produce a keyline. **FIGURE 7:7** shows a scan of film shot at 800 ISO sharpened with five different Radius/Threshold settings.

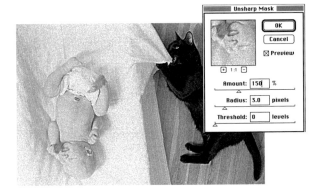

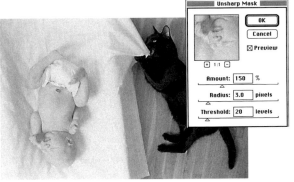

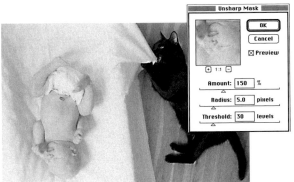

FIGURE 7:7

This photograph was shot with Kodak Tri-X film at 800 ISO, so it is inherently grainy. Higher Thresholds can prevent the grain from being exaggerated when this image is sharpened.

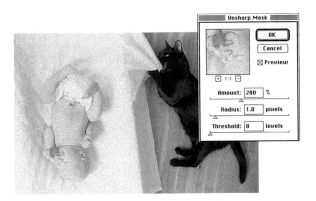

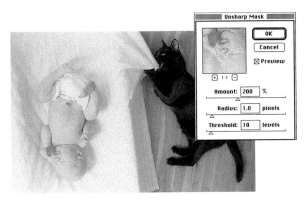

No sharpening

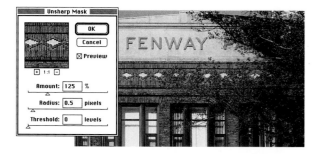

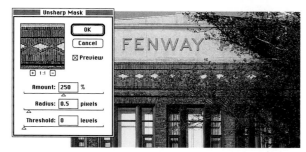

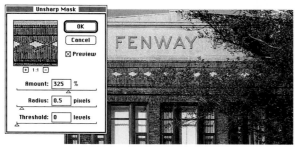

FIGURE 7:8

This photograph was shot with Ilford Delta 100 film at 100 ISO and has very little grain. In this case a low Radius and Threshold can be used to bring out more image detail.

If there is very little grain in the film to start with, a higher Amount and lower Radius and Threshold can be applied without the grain being revealed. **FIGURE 7:8** shows a scan of film shot at 100 ISO with three different Amount settings. In this case it is possible to reveal more image detail because there is less noise in the film to start with.

Scans of three-dimensional objects made from a flatbed scanner can be sharpened with even higher Amount and lower Radius and Threshold settings. In this case an extraordinary amount of detail can be revealed because there is no film grain (**FIGURE 7:9**).

If you scan three-dimensional objects there is no film grain and the lowest Radius and Threshold can be used along with very high Amounts. This feather was scanned directly on a Microtek 300Z flatbed.

FIGURE 7:9

LOCAL
CORRECTIONS

PHOTOSHOP PROVIDES A NUMBER of tools that let you adjust an image locally. You can make selections, and work on only the selected portions of the image while the rest of the image is masked. There are seven Photoshop tools that allow you to select part of an image, which I will cover later in Chapter Nine, *The Creative Pixel*. You can also use the painting tools—Eraser, Pencil, Brush, Airbrush, Rubber Stamp, Blur/Sharpen, and Dodge/Burn/Saturate—to make local color corrections to the picture. Using the painting tools to paint with is fairly intuitive; using them to color-correct an image is less obvious and I will cover those techniques in this chapter.

LOCAL SHARPENING

There are three steps to perform before using any of the painting or focus tools. You must select the tool by clicking on its icon in the tool box; select a brush from the Brushes palette (see **FIGURE 8:1**, *The Brushes Palette*); and choose the tool's attributes from the Options palette. The Sharpen tool also doubles as a Blur tool. You can Option-click on the tool icon to toggle between the Sharpen and Blur, or choose Sharpen or Blur from the Tools pop-up menu in the Focus Tools Options palette. The Dodge/Burn/Saturate tool also works in this manner.

After using the Unsharp Mask filter you may find that you want to sharpen specific parts of the scan further. You can use the Sharpen tool to sharpen areas such as hair or other fine details separately from the rest of the image. You can adjust the intensity of the Sharpen tool by changing the Pressure percentage in the Focus Tool Options palette (double-clicking on the tool opens the Options palette). The Pressure percentage can be adjusted from 1 to 100%. Simply choose a brush from the Brushes palette and paint on the sharpness. Typing the letter R is a shortcut for selecting the Focus tools. Press R again to toggle between Sharpen and Blur.

 A tool's Pressure, Opacity, or Exposure can be adjusted in 10% increments from the keyboard by pressing the number keys. Pressing 1 adjusts the percentage to 10%; pressing 2 adjusts the percentage to 20%; and so on.

TAKE SNAPSHOT

Using the Sharpen tool to sharpen specific parts of the image has the same kind of limitations that the Sharpen or Sharpen More filters have for overall sharpening. You cannot adjust the radius or threshold of the Sharpen tool as you can with the Unsharp Mask filter. You can, however, use the Rubber Stamp tool in combination with Take Snapshot to apply the Unsharp Mask filter to parts of an image with the Rubber Stamp tool.

The Brushes Palette

You can arrange and customize your brushes via the Brushes palette. Clicking on the arrow in the upper right-hand corner accesses a pop-up menu (FIGURE A) that allows you to customize the Brushes palette:

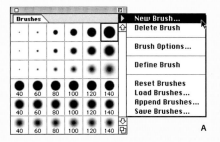

A

- Double-clicking on a brush or clicking once on a brush and choosing Brush Options allows you to adjust a brush stroke's diameter, hardness, spacing, angle, and roundness (FIGURE B).
- Choosing New Brush allows you to add a new brush to the palette. Delete Brush deletes the selected brush.
- Define Brush creates a brush from any currently selected pixels. This option is available only if there is an active selection.
- You can customize your Brushes palette, then save the customized palette by choosing Save Brushes. Then, to select a specific palette that you have saved, choose Load Brushes or Append brushes to combine two saved palettes.
- As you are painting you can avoid having to click on brushes by pressing the] or [keys—the] key selects the next brush in the palette moving left to right, and the [key selects brushes backwards through the palette.

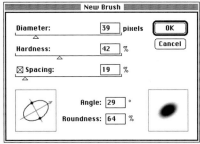

B

This can be very useful when a picture is noisy. For instance, if the scan is a portrait you might want to sharpen hair and facial features differently from smooth skin. You can apply an overall Unsharp Mask with a high Threshold setting to avoid accentuating noise in the smooth areas. An Unsharp Mask with a lower Radius and Threshold, and higher Amount, can then be applied to areas where noise is not as problematic, but where you want more definition in the fine details. Here is how to apply an Unsharp Mask using Take Snapshot:

1 Apply an Unsharp Mask filter with the desired setting to the entire image (**FIGURE 8:2**).

2 Choose Take Snapshot from the Edit menu (**FIGURE 8:3**). When you choose Take Snapshot, a copy of the image is stored, which can then be loaded into the Rubber Stamp tool.

3 Choose Undo Unsharp Mask (Command + Z) from the Edit menu (**FIGURE 8:4**).

4 You can now apply the Unsharp Mask you had specified before the undo to parts of the image by double-clicking on the Rubber Stamp tool and choosing From Snapshot from the Option pop-up menu in the Rubber Stamp Options palette. Clicking and dragging on the image with the Rubber Stamp paints on the Unsharp Mask (**FIGURE 8:5**). Adjusting the Rubber Stamp's Opacity setting lets you apply varying degrees of sharpness.

Apply the desired Unsharp Mask to the image.

FIGURE 8:2

Choose Take Snapshot from the Edit menu.

FIGURE 8:3

Undo the Unsharp Mask to revert back to the image as it was before applying the filter.

FIGURE 8:4

With the Rubber Stamp mode set to From Snapshot the Unsharp mask filter can be selectively applied to the image.

FIGURE 8:5

To define an entire image as a pattern, first duplicate it by choosing Duplicate from the Image menu.

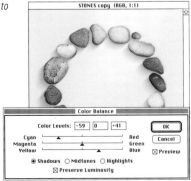

FIGURE 8:6

Make an adjustment to the duplicate file.

FIGURE 8:7

TAKE SNAPSHOT AND DEFINE PATTERN You can accomplish the same effect as Take Snapshot using Define Pattern. In this case you can have one effect loaded as a snapshot, and another effect loaded as a pattern; you can then apply the two effects by switching the Rubber Stamp Option between From Snapshot and Pattern (aligned). To define a pattern:

1 Choose Duplicate from the Image menu. The Duplicate Image dialog box appears. Click OK and a duplicate window appears (**FIGURE 8:6**).

2 Adjust the duplicate file by applying a filter or changing its color (**FIGURE 8:7**).

3 Choose All from the Select menu (Command+A) and then choose Define Pattern from the Edit menu (**FIGURE 8:8**). Choosing Define Pattern stores a copy of the adjusted duplicate window, which can be loaded as the Pattern (aligned) Option in the Rubber Stamp tool. You can now close the duplicate file without saving it.

Select the entire image and choose Define Pattern from the Edit menu.

FIGURE 8:8

4 Choose Pattern (aligned) as the Option in the Rubber Stamp Options palette. You can paint on the adjustments made to the duplicate file, at any Opacity setting (**FIGURE 8:9**).

FIGURE 8:10 shows part of the image being adjusted to blue using Define Pattern, while another part is adjusted to red using Take Snapshot. Remember, any effect you can apply to an image can be saved as a snapshot or pattern—so you could also load two different filter effects and apply them locally with the Rubber Stamp tool.

 Photoshop only has one level of undo. It is possible to create the equivalent of multiple levels of undo using the Define Pattern, Take Snapshot, and Revert to Save features. Choosing the From Saved Option in the Rubber Stamp Options palette lets you revert any part of the image to the last version saved. You can also make snapshots and define patterns at different stages as you work, allowing you to use the Rubber Stamp tool to move back steps. Keep in mind that both Take Snapshot and Define Pattern store copies of the image in memory or on the scratch disk, so you will need enough memory and disk space available to use these tools (see Appendix C, Faster Photoshop).

TONING TOOL You can adjust the lightness, darkness, and saturation of parts of an image using the Dodge, Burn, or Sponge tools. Option-clicking on the tool's icon in the tool box toggles among the three tools. The Dodge tool lightens where you click and drag while the Burn tool darkens. You can choose Shadows, Midtones, or Highlights as an option in the Toning Tool Options palette and you can choose an Exposure from 1% to 100%. Both the Dodge and Burn tools are fairly intense, so you will probably want to set the Exposure to less than 10%. When the Sponge

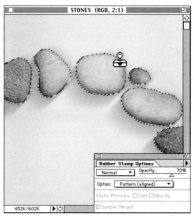

FIGURE 8:9

Choosing Pattern (aligned) from the Rubber Stamp Options palette lets you apply the defined pattern to the original image.

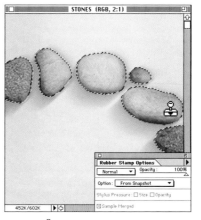

FIGURE 8:10

You can use the Define Pattern and Take Snapshot features to apply two different effects using the Rubber Stamp. Here, From Snapshot mode adds red to the image while Pattern (aligned) mode adds blue.

The Toner tools let you selectively darken, lighten, saturate, or desaturate parts of an image.

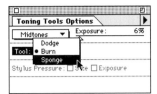

FIGURE 8:11

Option-clicking and then clicking and dragging again with the Rubber Stamp tool set to Clone lets you selectively copy areas from one part of the image to another.

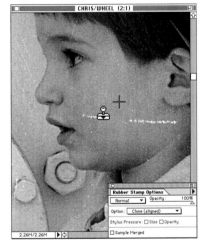

FIGURE 8:12

tool is selected, you can choose either Saturate or Desaturate as an option (**FIGURE 8:11**). Typing the letter O is a shortcut for selecting the Toning tools—pressing O more than once cycles through the three tools.

CLONING The Rubber Stamp tool also has a mode that lets you easily remove unwanted artifacts such as dust and scratches. The Clone (Aligned) and Clone (Non-aligned) Option of the Rubber Stamp tool lets you selectively pick up parts of the image and copy them back to another part of the image. Select Clone (aligned) and Option-click on the image, release the option key and click and drag on another part of the image, and the pixels that you first Option-clicked will be copied to the new area. The size of the copied area depends on the size of the brush you have chosen. As you click and drag a crosshair will appear above the area being copied from. With Clone (Aligned) chosen, the point being copied always remains aligned at the same distance from the point to which the pixels are being cloned. If Clone (Non-aligned) is chosen, the copy point remains aligned until you release the mouse button (**FIGURE 8:12**). Typing the letter S is a shortcut for selecting the Rubber Stamp tool.

> You can also use the smudge tool with its mode set to Darken in the Smudge Tool Options palette to remove small spots that are lighter than their background. Setting the mode to Lighten removes dark spots on a light background. For small spots this method is faster than cloning since you do not have to Option-click before smudging away the spot. Typing the letter U is a shortcut for selecting the Smudge tool.

GAMUT WARNING

When you have finished color-correcting, sharpening, and touching up an image, there is one final step before printing and that is converting to CMYK mode. High-end scanners usually make this conversion using their own software and the conversion is very important to the overall quality of the image (see **FIGURE 8:13**, *Comparing Scanners*). Getting output that is reasonably accurate to what you see on your display depends on the RGB to CMYK conversion, and that will be covered in Chapter Fifteen, *Color Management*.

When you work in RGB Mode, the color palette that is available to you is much broader than the palette of colors that is printable. The reasons for this will be covered in more detail in Chapter Fifteen, but you should be aware of the fact that the colors you choose in RGB Mode might be altered when they are converted to CMYK and printed. The complete palette of colors that is available in a given color mode is often referred to as the mode's gamut. When you are working in RGB Mode you can preview which colors are outside of the CMYK gamut in an image by choosing Gamut Warning from the Mode menu. When you choose Gamut Warning, the colors that will be adjusted when converting to CMYK Mode are temporarily overlayed with a colored mask. The color and transparency of the overlay can be set by choosing Gamut Warning from the Preferences submenu under Edit (**FIGURE 8:14**). To turn off the Gamut Warning, choose it again from the Mode menu.

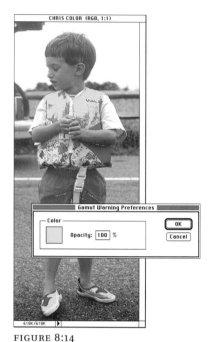

FIGURE 8:14

Turning on Gamut Warning temporarily indicates out-of-gamut colors with a color overlay.

 Photoshop 3.0's new Color Range selection tool allows you to specifically select out-of-gamut pixels and adjust them independently from the rest of the image. (See FIGURE 9:10, *Selecting by Color Range*.)

Comparing Scanners

Hell DCS 3010   **A**

Nikon 3500   **B**

Microtek 300Z   **C**

Photo CD   **D**

The capabilities of scanners vary depending on the model. FIGURES A, B, C and D show the results of the same 35 MM slide scanned on different scanners. FIGURE A was scanned on a Hell DCS-3010, an expensive high-end drum scanner. FIGURE B was scanned on a Nikon 3500 desktop slide scanner ($6,000). FIGURE C was scanned on a Microtek 300Z, an inexpensive flatbed scanner ($1,200). FIGURE D was acquired from a Kodak Photo CD. Photo CD is a service provided by Kodak and other vendors which allows you to have transparencies scanned and written to a CD-ROM disk for a relatively inexpensive price. Many photo labs now offer this service. Before scanning on the Microtek, I had the slide made into a high-quality 4 x 5 inch Cibachrome print. The high-end scan (FIGURE A) was converted into CMYK by the scanner's software (see Chapter Fifteen, *Color Management*). I color-corrected and used Photoshop's Unsharp Mask filter to sharpen the Nikon, Photo CD, and Microtek scans, then converted them to CMYK with Photoshop.

THE
CREATIVE
PIXEL
9

CHAPTER THREE SHOWED HOW THE image resolution of a Photoshop file is determined by the user. If the pixels are specified to be larger than the halftone dot, then the pixel will become visible when the image is printed. Showing the pixel is not always undesirable; it can be used to form beautiful patterns and textures, and there is the added benefit of relatively small file sizes. The marks made by the pixel can be reminiscent of mezzotint etching or woodcut, where the printmaker exploits the mark of the printmaking method. Woodcut printers often accentuate the wood's texture rather than attempting to hide it—the wood grain becomes a design element. In this chapter I will explore some ways of revealing the pixel and turning it into a desirable mark rather than an unwanted artifact.

THE PIXEL AND THE POSTER

Working on dimensionally large pieces in Photoshop can cause many problems. Consider the file size of an RGB image if it is 17 x 22 inches and 300 pixels per inch—96.3 megabytes. The same file at 72 pixels per inch is 5.55 megabytes. If you were to add extra channels and layers (see Chapter Twelve, *Layers*) to the 96.3 MB file, the file size could easily triple—not a pleasant prospect on most desktop computers.

The first example of an effective use of the pixel that I will show is a poster Lance Hidy designed for a one-man show of his work at the Corcoran Gallery of Art in Washington D.C. (**FIGURE 9:1**). Lance studied printmaking and graphic design at Yale, and has worked professionally as a book designer, poster artist, and photographer. The Corcoran poster's final output size was 17 x 22 inches at 72 ppi.

He created the Corcoran poster from two scanned slides taken from his photo archive—one of Michelangelo's, *Dying Slave*, and the other of tree limbs against a cloudy sky (**FIGURE 9:2**). The poster art was created by silhouetting the tree limbs against a white background, then selecting the statue and cutting and pasting it behind the limbs.

 When creating art where the pixel is intentionally shown, make sure that the pixels are big enough. If the pixels get too small the halftone dots of the printed page can no longer define the pixels clearly. FIGURE 9:3 shows a portion of the poster at 100% of the printed size so that you can see the texture of the pixels as they appeared in the finished poster. If the image resolution is much higher than 80 ppi the pixels get difficult to see.

FIGURE 9:1

FIGURE 9:2

Lance started with two 35 mm slides scanned on a Nikon LS 3500 slide scanner.

FIGURE 9:3

This enlarged section of the poster shows the pixel texture at 100%.

Selection Modifiers

There are seven additional Select menu items that let you modify an existing selection:

- **FEATHER:** To soften the edge of a selection, choose Feather. You can choose a Feather Radius of up to 250 pixels (FIGURE A).
- **BORDER:** To convert the edges of a selection into a selected border, choose Border from the Modify submenu. The width of the border can be up to 64 pixels (FIGURE B).
- **SMOOTH:** To round the corners of a selection, choose Smooth from the Modify submenu. The Sample Radius can be up to 16 pixels (FIGURE C).
- **EXPAND AND CONTRACT:** Choose Expand (FIGURE D) or Contract (FIGURE E) from the Modify submenu to expand or contract a selection in 1 pixel increments up to 16 pixels.
- **GROW:** To expand a selection based on the pixel values at the edges of the selection, choose Grow. The Tolerance setting in the Magic Wand Options palette affects how much the selection will grow.
- **SIMILAR:** To select all the other pixels in the image of similar value, choose Similar. The Tolerance setting in the Magic Wand Options palette effects how similar in value the added pixels will be.

The unmodified selection

A

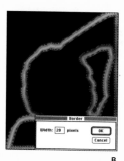

B

C

D

E

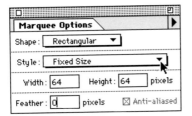

FIGURE 9:5

You can choose to constrain the aspect ratio of an elliptical or rectangular selection, or you can fix its size, by clicking on the Marquee Options palette's Style pop-up menu.

THE SELECTION TOOLS

Before combining imagery from various sources you must first learn how to make selections. Photoshop has seven tools designed for selecting parts of an image—the Rectangular/Elliptical Marquee, Lasso, Magic Wand, Pen, Color Range, and Quick Mask tools. There are also other menu items for modifying a selection (see **FIGURE 9:4**, *Selection Modifiers*). Once part of an image is selected, it can be worked on independently from the nonselected parts of the image. A selected area is indicated by a dotted line moving around its edges. Below is an overview of Photoshop's selection tools.

RECTANGULAR AND ELLIPTICAL   The top left-hand icon in the tool box represents the most basic selection tools, the Rectangular and Elliptical marquees. Option-clicking on the tool's icon toggles between the two shapes. They allow you to quickly click and drag out rectangular, square, circular, and elliptical selections. Double-clicking on either icon opens the Marquee Options palette that allows you to specify exact pixel dimensions or aspect ratios for a selection. Clicking on the Style pop-up menu lets you choose Constrained Aspect Ratio or Fixed size. Choosing one of these enables the Width and Height box (**FIGURE 9:5**). Typing the letter M is a shortcut for selecting the Rectangular or Elliptical Marquee tool.

FIGURE 9:6

Holding down the Option key while you use the Lasso tool lets you release the mouse button, pull out straight selections, and then click to anchor them.

LASSO   The Lasso tool is used for making manual, irregular selections. You draw the selection freehand, which can be difficult with a mouse, so it takes some practice. By clicking and dragging, you can create a selection line around any area of the image. When you release the mouse button, the two ends of the lasso line are automatically connected. This can be frustrating if you accidentally release the mouse button. However, with the Option key pressed, you can release the mouse button without the selection being automatically completed. Also, if you move the mouse with the button released and the Option key pressed, a straight line is pulled out that can be anchored with a click of the mouse button. This is an effective way to select hard-edged shapes (**FIGURE 9:6**). Typing the letter L is a shortcut for selecting Lasso tool.

 Sometimes, after drawing a selection, you may want to add or subtract areas from a selection. If you want to add to a current selection, hold down the Shift key and make an additional selection. The new selection will be added to the

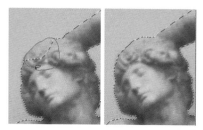

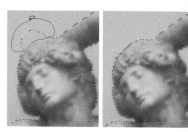

Holding down the Shift key lets you add to a selection (A). Holding down the Command key lets you take away part of a selection (B). Holding down Command + Shift lets you intersect an existing selection, eliminating all but intersected parts of the selection (C).

FIGURE 9:7   C

The selection marquee of complex selections can be distracting; choose Hide Edges (Command+H) from the Select menu to toggle the marquee on and off.

FIGURE 9:8

existing selection. If you want to subtract from a selection, hold down the Command key; whatever you draw that intersects with an existing selection will be removed from the selection. Holding down both the Command and Shift keys lets you intersect an existing selection with a new selection, and only the intersected part of the two selections will remain selected (**FIGURE 9:7**).

MAGIC WAND   The Magic Wand is used for automatically selecting contiguous areas of an image that have similar value and color. Double-clicking on the icon opens a dialog box that allows you to set a tolerance. If you increase the Tolerance number, then more values will be added to the selection; the default is 32 with Anti-aliased checked. Checking Anti-aliased makes the edge of the selection smoother. Typing the letter W is a shortcut for selecting the Magic Wand tool.

⚠ CAUTION **The currently selected part of an image is surrounded by a moving marquee, which can be distracting, particularly with complex selections such as those created by the Magic Wand tool. Choose Hide Edges (Command + H) from the Select menu to temporarily hide the selection marquee—but be careful you don't forget that there is a hidden selection. Choose Show Edges (Command + H) to make the selection marquee show again (FIGURE 9:8).**

PEN TOOL   The Pen tool allows you to draw very accurate selections made with straight lines and curves, called bezier curves, that have anchor and control points (see **FIGURE 9:9**, *The Paths Palette*). You can then select the anchor and control points and manipulate them to adjust the path at anytime. If you are familiar with drawing programs such as Adobe Illustrator and Aldus Freehand, this tool will

The Paths Palette

With the Pen tool you can create very precise hard-edged selections which can be saved and loaded when needed. The Pen tool is located in the Paths palette—choose Show Paths from the Palettes submenu under Window (see accompanying figure). Clicking on the Pen tool (1) makes it active. If you have used other drawing programs such as Adobe Illustrator, the Pen tool and its Bezier curves will be familiar to you. If you have never drawn with Bezier curves, read the section on the Pen tool in the *Adobe Photoshop User Guide*. Here is an overview of the Paths palette's tools and menus:

- **PATH SELECT TOOL** (2): With the Path Select tool selected, you can click and drag on a path's anchor points or segments to move them. Holding down the Option key while you click and drag will copy the entire path. Holding down the Option+Command keys turns the Path Select tool into the Add Point tool—clicking on a line segment adds an anchor point to the segment. If you place the cursor on an existing anchor point, the cursor becomes the Delete Point tool and clicking deletes the anchor point from the path. If you are using the Pen tool you can access the Path Select tool by holding down the Command key.

- **ADD POINT TOOL** (3): With the Add Point tool active you can click on a section to add an anchor point. If the cursor is on top of an existing anchor point it becomes the Arrow tool and clicking and dragging moves the point. Holding down the Control key changes the cursor to the Delete Point tool when it is on top of an anchor point—clicking eliminates that point. Holding down the Command+Control lets you convert a corner point to a smooth point.

- **DELETE POINT TOOL** (4): With the Delete Point tool active you can click on an anchor point and eliminate it from the path. If the cursor is on top of the path but not an anchor point, it becomes the Path Select tool and clicking and dragging moves the segment. Holding down the Control key changes the cursor to the Add Point tool when it is on top of a segment—clicking adds an anchor point.

- **CORNER TOOL** (5): Use the Corner tool to convert a smooth point to a corner point, or click and drag on a corner point to make it smooth.

Click on the arrow in the Paths palette's upper right-hand corner to access more Path options:

- **PALETTE OPTIONS:** Choose Palette Options to select the size of the previews displayed in the palette.

- **NEW PATH:** Choose New Path to start work on a new path. The New Path dialog lets you name the path. You can also double-click the New Paths icon (6) to create a new path.

- **DUPLICATE PATH:** Make a path active by clicking on its name in the palette and choose Duplicate Path to make a copy of the path. You can also copy a path by dragging it into the New Paths icon (6).

- **DELETE PATH:** To delete a path, click on its name and choose Delete Path, or click on its name and drag it into the Trash icon (7).

- **TURN OFF PATH:** Choose Turn Off Path to deactivate a path, or click once in the palette under the list of paths.

- **MAKE PATH:** Choose Make Path to turn a selection into a path. The Make Path dialog box lets you assign a Tolerance from 0.5 to 10—the lower the number the more anchor points will be used to make the path. If there is a selection and no paths are turned on, then you can click on the Make Selection icon (8) to convert the selection to a path. Holding down the option key when you click lets you assign a Tolerance.

- **MAKE SELECTION:** To convert a path into a selection, click on its name in the palette and choose Make Selection. The Make Selection dialog box lets you convert the path into a new selection or add to, subtract from, or intersect it with an existing selection. Clicking on the Make Selection icon (8) converts an active path to a selection and holding down the Option key as you click accesses the Make Selection dialog box. You can also press the Enter key while the Pen tool is selected to convert a path to a selection.

- **FILL PATH:** Choose Fill Path to fill a path. The Fill Path dialog box's Use pop-up menu lets you choose to fill with the Foreground or Background color. You can also choose to revert the contents of the path to the last saved version of the file, or the fill can be from a Take Snapshot or Define Pattern. Click on the Fill Path icon (9) to fill a path with the Foreground color; holding down the Option key as you click accesses the Fill Path dialog box.

- **STROKE PATH:** Choose Stroke Path to stroke the path with the Foreground color using any of the painting tools. The way the stroke is applied is determined by the size of the brush set for the tool in the Brushes palette, and the options set for the tool in the tool's Options palette. Clicking on the Stroke Path (10) icon strokes the path with the currently active tool; holding down the Option key as you click accesses the Stroke Path dialog box.

- **CLIPPING PATH:** Choosing Clipping Path lets you designate a path from the Path pop-up menu, which will clip away the image's background when it is placed in another program.

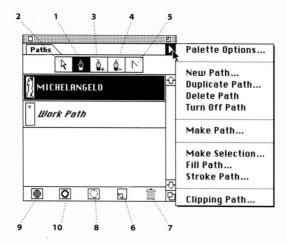

Selecting by Color Range

Color Range is a selection tool new to Photoshop 3.0 found in the Select menu. It is very similar in concept to Replace Color (FIGURE 6:20). Color Range lets you build a mask based on the primary colors, shadows, highlights, neutrals, or by colors sampled from the image. Choose a mode from the Select pop-up menu in the Color Range dialog box. If you choose Sampled Colors, you can click on pixels in the image to create the selection mask. The mask's white areas are representative of the selection you will get when you click OK. You have your choice of showing a preview of the image, or the mask by clicking on the Image or Selection radio buttons. If you choose Selection, then also choose None from the Selection Preview pop-up menu; in this case you will see the mask in the dialog box and the image's window will be unaffected (FIGURE A).

A

You can build the mask by choosing Sampled Colors from the Select pop-up menu, clicking anywhere on the image, and then adjusting the Fuzziness slider to expand the mask as necessary. Click on the Eyedropper+ icon to add other pixel values to the mask, or click on the Eyedropper– icon to click and contract the mask. Holding down the shift key as you click is a shortcut to the Eyedropper+ tool; holding down the Command key accesses the Eyedropper– tool. Using the Eyedropper+ tool and adjusting Fuzziness lets you quickly select specific areas in the image (FIGURE B).

B

You can also choose to show the mask on the image and preview the image in the dialog box by clicking the Preview radio button and choose viewing mode from the Selection Preview pop-up menu (FIGURE C).

C

Setting the Crop tool to a specific Width, Height, and Resolution resizes and resamples the image as it is cropped.

FIGURE 9:11

be easy to use. You access the Pen tool via the Paths palette—choose Show Paths from the Palettes submenu under Window. Clicking and dragging lays down anchor and control points that allow you to create straight lines and smooth curves. Any path you create can be saved with the file and and converted into a selection at any time. Typing the letter T is a shortcut for selecting the Pen tool.

COLOR RANGE   Choosing Color Range from the Select menu opens a dialog box that looks very similar to the Replace Color dialog box (**FIGURE 6:20**). In this case the black and white mask you see in the dialog box represents the areas of the image that will be selected when you click OK. For more on Color Range, see **FIGURE 9:10**, *Selecting by Color Range.*

 Another way of making selections is with the Quick Mask tool, which is covered in Chapter Ten, *Masks and Channels.*

CREATING A BITMAP

Lance started the Corcoran poster by resizing, and then converting the scan of the tree limbs to a black only bitmap. To make the tree bitmap:

1 He double-clicked on the Crop tool, checked Fixed Target Size in the Crop Tool Options dialog box, entered a Width and Height of 15 × 22.25 inches, and a Resolution of 72 ppi. He cropped the scan and it was resized and resampled (**FIGURE 9:11**).

2 Using the Levels tool (Command + L), he moved the black and white point Output sliders inward until the tree limbs were almost pure black on a white background (**FIGURE 9:12**).

3 There were still unwanted remnants of gray sky that Lance removed using Photoshop 3.0's Replace Color feature. He chose Replace Color from the Adjust submenu under Image. He moved the Lightness slider under Transform all the way to the right (this ensured that the affected pixels would be converted to white). Selecting the Eyedropper+ tool he started clicking on unwanted gray values which were converted to white. Moving the Tolerance slider to the right he could expand the areas of gray that were affected (**FIGURE 9:13**).

4 Finally Lance chose Threshold (Command + T) from the Map submenu under Image. Threshold converts the pixels to black and white only (**FIGURE 9:14**).

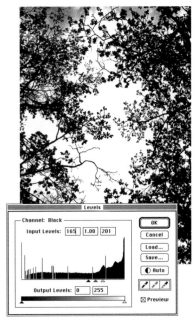

Using Levels, Lance adjusted the image until the limbs were black and the sky was mostly white.

FIGURE 9:12

Lance used Replace Color to remove the unwanted gray values in the sky.

FIGURE 9:13

Threshold converts the grayscale image to black and white only.

FIGURE 9:14

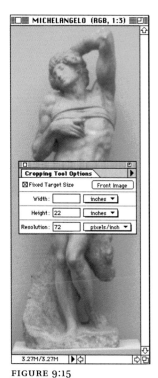

FIGURE 9:15

Leaving Width blank in the Crop Tool Options palette let Lance crop to a specific height and resolution without constraining the aspect ratio of the dimensions.

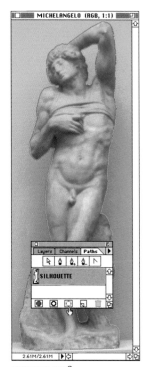

FIGURE 9:16

Clicking on the Selection icon at the bottom of the Paths palette converts the targeted path to a selection.

CUTTING AND PASTING

With the bitmapped tree limbs complete, Lance opened and cropped the scan of the statue. In this case he set the Crop tool's options to 22 inches in the Height box, 72 ppi in the Resolution box, and he left the Width box blank. He used this setting because he wanted the resolution and the height to match that of the tree limbs. He left Width blank so that the crop marquee would not be proportionally constrained (**FIGURE 9:15**).

Lance used the Pen tool to select the statue from its background. A pen path converts to a very crisp, hard-edged selection, which Lance was looking for in this case. To convert the path to a selection, he clicked on the selection icon in the Paths palette (**FIGURE 9:16**) and then made a copy of the selection (Command + C). Having selected and copied the statue, Lance could now paste it behind the tree limbs:

1 First Lance converted the tree limbs to RGB mode by choosing RGB Color from the Mode menu (**FIGURE 9:17**). If he had copied the statue,

Pasting a color image into a grayscale image converts the color of the pasted image to grayscale, so Lance changed the mode of the branches to RGB before pasting the statue.

FIGURE 9:17

which was in RGB mode into the grayscale tree limbs, its color would have been converted to grayscale.

2 He double-clicked on the Magic Wand and set its Tolerance to 0 and left Anti-aliased unchecked in the Magic Wand Options palette. This setting ensures that only pixels of one value will be selected. He then clicked on an area of the white sky—the white pixel clicked on, and all the adjoining white pixels were automatically selected (**FIGURE 9:18**). If the Magic Wand selects more than one pixel color when it is set to a Tolerance of 0, double-click the Eyedropper tool and make sure the Sample Size is set to Point sample.

3 To select the other areas of white sky, Lance chose Similar from the Select menu (**FIGURE 9:19**).

4 Lance chose Paste Into from the Edit menu, which pasted the copied statue behind the trees (or *into* the sky). If he had chosen Paste (Command + V) from the Edit menu the statue would have been pasted on top of the trees (**FIGURE 9:20**). If you hold down the Option key while choosing Paste Into, the copied selection is pasted behind the current selection instead.

Setting the Magic Wand's tolerance to 0 and unchecking Anti-aliased ensures that only pixels of one value are selected—white in this case.

FIGURE 9:18

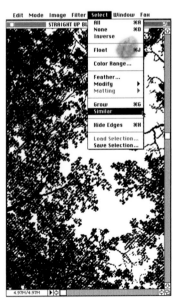

FIGURE 9:19

Lance chose Similar from the Select menu to select the remaining white pixels.

Choosing Paste Into pastes a copied image into a selection.

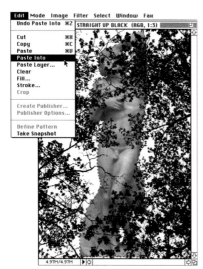

FIGURE 9:20

The Scale tool lets you adjust the size of a floating selection.

FIGURE 9:21

5 The statue was too large so Lance adjusted its size by choosing Scale from the Effects submenu under Image (**FIGURE 9:21**). When you choose Scale, a small square appears at each corner of the current selection. Clicking and dragging on the squares allows you to adjust the size of the selection. Holding down the Shift key forces the scaling to be proportional. Clicking inside the selection marquee makes the final scale (see **FIGURE 9:22**, *Effects and Rotations*).

6 Lance could also adjust the statue's position by selecting the Move tool and clicking and dragging inside the selection. Holding down the Command key also lets you move a selection when another tool is active.

 For a novice Photoshop user, cutting an image from one window and pasting it into another can often produce unexpected results. You might cut and paste what appears to be a small object into a larger window, only to have the object seemingly enlarge itself, and overflow the new window. For cutting and pasting purposes only pixel dimensions are considered—not the output dimensions (see **FIGURE 9:23**, *Pasting and Resolution*).

Lance converted the finished piece to CMYK and saved it as an EPS file. He used the EPS format so that the file could be placed in Adobe Illustrator where the type was added. For more on exporting Photoshop files to other programs, see Appendix A, *File Formats*.

Effects and Rotations

A

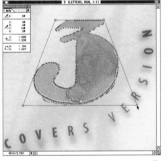

B

You can alter the size and shape of a selected area by choosing any of the items in the Rotate or Effects submenus under Image. You can choose to rotate the selected pixels 180°, 90° cw (clockwise), 90° ccw (counterclockwise), or if you choose Arbitrary you can designate an exact rotation by degree. Choose Free if you want to visually rotate the selection. When you choose Free small squares appear at the corners of the selection. Click and drag on the squares to turn the selection. After rotating the selection in this manner, a preview of the rotated pixels appears—when you are satisfied with the selection's position, click inside the marquee to make the final rotation (FIGURE A). If there is is no active selection, then the entire image with all of its layers will be rotated.

The items in the Effects menu work in a similar manner. Scale lets you resize a selection—hold down the Shift key to constrain the proportions (FIGURE B). Skew, Perspective, and Distort allow you to distort the selection accordingly (FIGURES C–E). When you resize or distort a selection the selected area is resampled. If possible, always paste the selection larger than needed, and then scale the selection down.

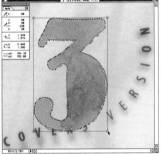

C

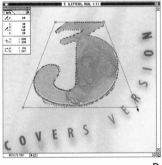

D

E

Pasting and Resolution

A

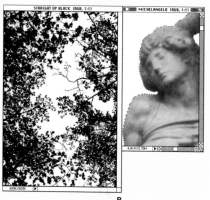

B

FIGURE A shows what can happen if you attempt to paste a high-resolution image into a low-resolution window. To ensure that a cut or pasted object pastes at the proper size into another window:

1 Preview the window that you want to paste into along-side the window with the selection that you are cutting or copying from.

2 Typing Command + + or Command + - increases or decreases the preview size of the active window; the ratio in the title bar changes accordingly. Adjust one or both windows until the title bar ratios are the same (FIGURE B).

3 If the selection that you plan to copy appears to be larg-er than the window it is being pasted into, you should resize it. Click on its title bar and choose Image Size from the Image menu. With Proportions checked and File Size unchecked, enter a lower resolution or dimen-sion. Click OK and the window size will become smaller while its ratio stays the same (FIGURE C). When you resize the image, any current selection will be lost, so resize before you make the selection.

4 You can now make a selection, copy it, and it will paste inside of the destination window's border (FIGURE D).

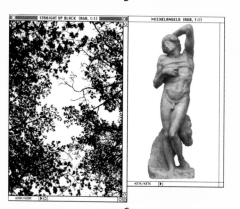

C

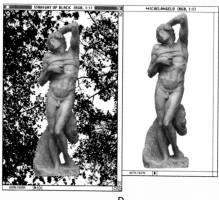

D

DESELECTING

When you paste a selection that you have cut or copied, the selection is referred to as a floating selection (**FIGURE 9:24**). As long as a selection is floating it can be moved without effecting the underlying image. When you deselect the floating selection, by choosing None (Command + D) from the Select menu, you permanently paste down the floating pixels and destroy the underlying pixels. Photoshop 3.0 remedies this inconvenience with the new Layers feature, which allows you to have pixels on separate layers within one document (see Chapter Twelve, *Layers*). Here are some important things to know about selections and floating selections:

- Clicking inside of a window that has a floating selection will deselect and permanently paste the floating selection into its layer if the Crop, Type, or any of the selection tools active.

- If one of the selection tools is active, you can move an existing selection by holding down the Option+Command keys and clicking and dragging inside the selection. If the selection is floating, its pixels are pasted and only the selection marquee moves.

- If the selection is floating, holding down the Command key and intersecting the floating selection with a new selection deletes that part of the floating selection and its pixels. If both the Command and Shift keys are held down everything but the area intersected is deleted (**FIGURE 9:25**).

- You can paste down part of a floating selection and leave the remaining selection floating by selecting the Type tool, holding down the Command key (the Type icon is converted into a

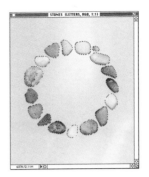

The pixels of a floating selection do not replace the underlying image's pixels until the floating selection is deselected.

FIGURE 9:24

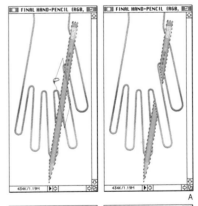
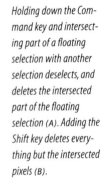

Holding down the Command key and intersecting part of a floating selection with another selection deselects, and deletes the intersected part of the floating selection (A). Adding the Shift key deletes everything but the intersected pixels (B).

A

B

FIGURE 9:25

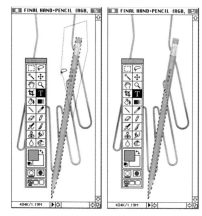

FIGURE 9:26

Lasso), and selecting the part of the floating selection you want to paste down (**FIGURE 9:26**)

- If you make a selection and move it by clicking and dragging inside the selection (while a selection tool is active, or while holding down the Command key), the moved pixels will be replaced with the current background color or, if there is more than one layer, the pixels of the underlying layer will show through. If you also hold down the Option key before making the move, a copy of the selected area is moved and the underlying pixels are left unaltered.

- You can also make a copy of an existing selection by choosing Float (Command+J) from the Select menu. In this case a copy of the selected area is floated on top of the image without altering the underlying pixels.

BITMAP TEXTURES

You can use the pixel to create visually appealing textures and surfaces. **FIGURE 9:27** shows a series of book jackets on baseball that I illustrated for Creative Education of Mankato, Minnesota. In this case I used the pixels as a mark that created the texture I was looking for. There was also a practical reason for using the pixel in this manner—the art for the jackets had to be 16.5 x 11 inches and there would be 26 jackets. Fully resolved art would have had file sizes of between 25 and 50 megabytes each. At 65 ppi, which was the resolution I used, the file size was 2.25 MB—a much more manageable file on the 8 MB Macintosh II that I was using at the time (**FIGURE 9:28**).

FIGURE 9:27

A series of books on baseball for junior high students published by Creative Education. Design by Virginia Evans and art direction by Rita Marshall.

I used the pixel to create a texture for the baseball series cover illustrations. The 16.5 x 11 inch illustrations were only 2.25 megabytes. The inset shows the pixel texture at 100%.

FIGURE 9:28

DITHERED BITMAPS   I started the project by scanning black and white stock photographs from the Bettman Archives as grayscale. I set the Cropping Tool Options to a Width and Height of 16.5 x 11 inches and a Resolution of 65 ppi and and cropped the scans (**FIGURE 9:29**). After cropping and adjusting the scan's brightness and contrast I created colored dithered bitmaps. To make colored bitmaps:

1 I chose Bitmap from the Mode menu (the file's mode must be grayscale for Bitmap to be available in the Mode menu). In the Bitmap dialog box I left 65 ppi as the Output Resolution, clicked on the Diffusion Dither radio button, and clicked OK. The grayscale image was converted to a dithered bitmap which is a pattern of randomly spaced pixels (**FIGURE 9:30**). The dithered

The artwork started with black and white stock photos from the Bettman Archives.

FIGURE 9:29

The grayscale scans were converted to diffusion dithered bitmaps.

FIGURE 9:30

bitmap is similar to stochastic screening where tonality is achieved by spacing same-sized dots at various distances (FIGURE 1:4).

2 The Bitmap mode is black and white only (it is 8 times smaller in file size than the grayscale image) and I wanted to color the pixels, so I converted the file back to grayscale mode, and then chose RGB Color from the Mode menu.

3 Once in RGB mode, I chose Color Range from the Select menu. I chose Shadows from the Select pop-up menu and clicked OK. All of the black pixels were selected and I could now adjust their color (FIGURE 9:31). This is a faster method of selecting the black pixels than using the Magic Wand and Select Similar.

4 At the bottom of Photoshop's tool box is a black box overlapping a white box. The foreground black box is used for choosing a foreground color; the background white box is for selecting

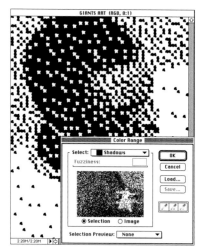

Color Range under the Select menu lets you quickly select all the black pixels of a black and white bitmap.

FIGURE 9:31

Choosing Color

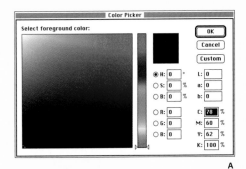

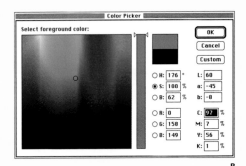

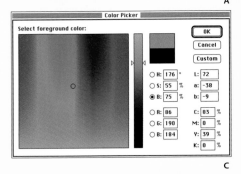

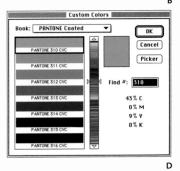

Photoshop provides a number of options for choosing color. Open the Color Picker by clicking on either the black or white square at the bottom of the tool box menu. The black square is for the foreground color and the white square is for the background color. FIGURE A shows the default color picker. Typing D is a shortcut for loading the default black and white colors; typing X swaps the colors.

The largest square shows hue with white added on the horizontal axis and black added on the vertical axis. You can change hue by moving the triangle to the right of the box up or down along the rainbow colored bar. The colored boxes to the right of the hue slider show the existing color on the bottom and the new color at the top.

Clicking and dragging inside of the large box changes the new color to correspond to the color beneath the cursor—or you can enter any desired CMYK percentage in the boxes at the far right. Clicking on the S, B, R, G, or B radio buttons gives variations on the default color picker. FIGURES B and C show the S and B pickers.

Once you have chosen a color, you can click on Custom to access a variety of custom color systems such as Pantone or Trumatch (FIGURE D). The color that you chose in the Color Picker is the color selected in the custom system or its closest match. Also, if you choose a new color from the custom color selector and then click on Picker, you return to the Photoshop Color Picker and the custom color that you chose will be selected.

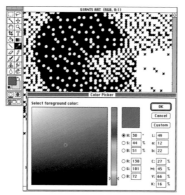

FIGURE 9:33

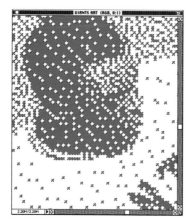

FIGURE 9:34

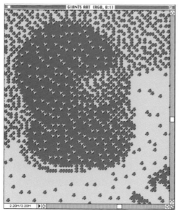

FIGURE 9:35

FIGURE 9:36

a background color. I clicked on the foreground box. This opens Photoshop's Color Picker (see **FIGURE 9:32**, *Choosing Color*). I chose a color and clicked OK (**FIGURE 9:33**).

5 I pressed Option + Delete, and the selected black pixels were filled with the foreground color (**FIGURE 9:34**). I could have also chosen Fill from the Edit menu.

6 With the black pixels colored, I inverted the selection by choosing Inverse from the Select menu, chose a new foreground color, and repeated step 5 to color the white pixels (**FIGURE 9:35**).

7 Finally I chose Add Noise from the Noise submenu under Filter. I set the Amount to 30 pixels, Distribution as Uniform, checked the Monochromatic box, and clicked OK. Applying the noise filter made the texture of the dithered bitmap less uniform (**FIGURE 9:36**)

NOTE You can also use dithered bitmaps to avoid the coarseness of halftone dots when printing from low-resolution printers like laser printers. This can be very effective if the image is high contrast and has fine details (see **FIGURE 9:37**, *Printing with Dithered Bitmaps*).

I chose fairly neutral colors to color the bitmap's pixels, and then used the painting tools to add color to the players. Using the Take Snapshot feature, and the Airbrush and Brush tools set at different coloring modes (see **FIGURE 9:38**, *Color Modes*), I could subtly add color to the illustrations (**FIGURE 9:39**).

MIXING RESOLUTIONS If you want to cut and paste a fully resolved element into an image where you have purposefully shown the pixel, and still maintain its higher resolution and size, you will have to first increase the resolution of the lower-resolution file to accommodate the pasted elements. In the case of the baseball jackets I wanted to add Illustrator drawings with texture as a placeholder for the titles (see Chapter Thirteen, *Importing from Illustrator*). In order to maintain the detail of the textures, the imported drawings needed more resolution than the 65 ppi Photoshop files.

Printing with Dithered Bitmaps

Because there must be enough printer resolution (dpi) available to accurately draw the different sized halftone dots (lpi), a 300 dpi laser printer is limited to about 60 lpi if there is to be any tonal variation in a picture (FIGURE 1:14). Such a coarse halftone screen is quite noticeable, and highly detailed images do not print well. You can bypass the halftone dot and produce a pseudo-stochastic screen (FIGURE 1:4) from a laser printer. Images with fine detail and high contrast will look much better in this case. Here's how to print a pseudo-stochastic screened image:

1 Start by sampling a grayscale image to a resolution of 300 ppi. The image resolution must be the same or exactly half the dpi resolution of your printer—if your printer's resolution is 600 dpi, the image resolution can be either 600 or 300 ppi.

2 The grayscale image will be converted to a dithered bitmap; but first the grayscale must be adjusted, otherwise the shadow areas will fill in when it is printed as a bitmap. FIGURE A shows the curve I apply that gives good results from my printer (in this case the horizontal input axis is set showing white on the left; for more on the Curves tool, see FIGURE 6:13). The curve makes the image look lighter and washed out as a grayscale, but it will look correct when converted to a bitmap and printed. You can start with a curve that looks like this and adjust it if necessary depending on the results from your printer.

3 Make sure to save the curve you use, by clicking the Save button in the Curves dialog box. When you click Save you can name the curve and save it to disk; the curve can then be loaded later by

opening Curves and clicking the Load button.

4 After applying the curve adjustment, choose Bitmap from the Mode menu. Leave the output resolution as 300 pixels/inch; choose Diffusion Dither as the Method. Click OK (FIGURE B).

5 The bitmapped image is one-eighth the size of the grayscale and no halftone dot will be used when you print, since the pixel values are only black or white. FIGURE C shows the 300 dpi bitmap compared to a grayscale printed at 56 lpi.

 It is wise to apply the curve and bitmap to a duplicate grayscale image, since it is impossible to convert the bitmap back in to gray values. Images with detail and good contrast work best with this method, while images with soft edges and subtle tonal shifts do not work as well. If you export the bitmap to another program it cannot be resized, since the bitmap resolution would no longer match the resolution of the printer, which is essential if the image is to look good.

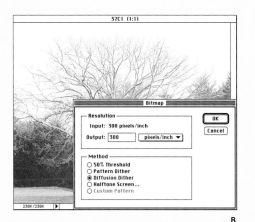

B

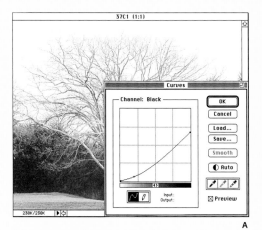

A

C

Color Modes

The painting tools can be used with a variety of color modes. The mode you choose from a tool's Option palette (FIGURE A) determines how the painted color interacts with the image's pixels. For instance, if you choose Darken, only pixels with a lighter value than the painted color will be affected. FIGURE B shows the same image with various colored paint strokes applied using different modes.

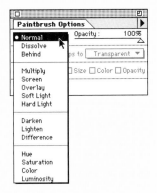

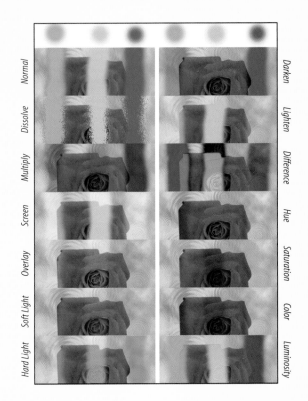

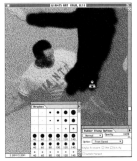 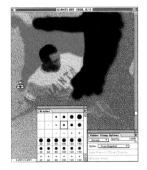 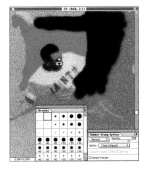 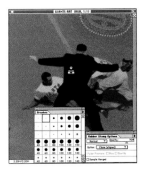

FIGURE 9:39

I added color to the illustrations by adjusting the overall color, choosing Take Snapshot, Undo, and then painting with the Rubber Stamp tool at various opacities.

Pasting the 130 ppi sticker into the 65 ppi background caused the sticker to double in size.

FIGURE 9:40

If I had copied a drawing with twice as much resolution, it would have doubled in size when pasted into the lower resolution file (**FIGURE 9:40**). If I sampled up the files using Photoshop's default Bicubic Interpolation method, then the edges of the pixels became blurred (**FIGURE 9:41**). I prevented this fuzziness by changing the General Preferences Interpolation setting to Nearest Neighbor, and increasing the resolution by whole number multiples. In this case I doubled the resolution to 130 pixels per inch, but I could also have used other multiples—185, 270, and so on. After sampling up using this method, the image appeared the same, but the resolution had doubled and I could now paste the Illustrator drawing at the correct size and at a higher resolution (**FIGURE 9:42**).

FIGURE 9:41

Increasing the resolution of a pixelated image using Bicubic Interpolation causes the pixels to blur and appear out of focus.

Some imagesetters and printers adjust a file's image resolution during output. This resampling can be very bad for images where you want to retain a crisp hard-edged pixel, as it will blur the pixels as shown in FIGURE 9:41. Two commonly used output devices that upsample low-resolution files are Scitex imagesetters and Iris inkjet printers. Always test an output device before sending pixelated images for output.

FIGURE 9:42

After doubling the resolution using Nearest Neighbor interpolation, the file appeared identical, but could now accommodate the 130 ppi sticker without changing its size.

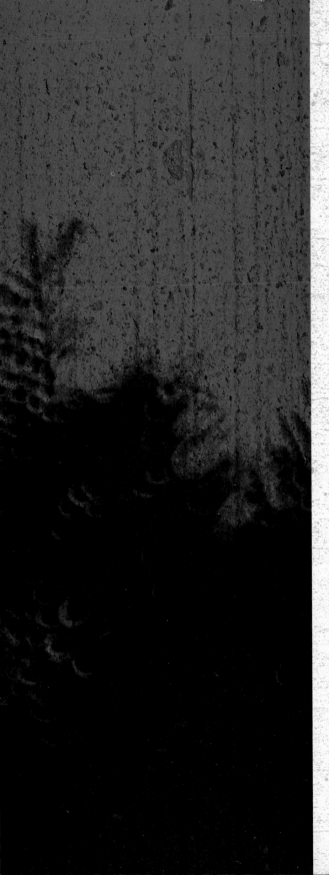

MASKS
AND
CHANNELS

10

Masks are a sophisticated way of controlling and manipulating specific areas of an image. They can be used for straightforward tasks such as saving a selection that has been time-consuming to create, or they can be used for more complex image editing tasks. With masks, you can create subtle blends and color shifts within images, or regulate how a filter affects a specific part of an image. When Photoshop was first released, masks were called alpha channels. Version 2.0 dropped the term alpha channel for the more user-friendly Save Selection and Load Selection, but you may still hear the term alpha channel used.

There are analogies in traditional graphic arts to Photoshop's masks. Printers use rubyliths to mask or silhouette photographs and art when preparing them for reproduction. Photoshop's Quick Mask feature covered later in this chapter is a direct analogy to the rubylith. Silkscreen printing provides another analogy in the way it employs masks or stencils to block parts of a screen and leave other parts open for ink to pass through onto paper (FIGURE 10:1).

CHANNELS

Every RGB Photoshop file has three channels, one for each of the RGB colors, and a full-color preview that you use for editing the image (FIGURE 10:2). If you select part of the image, the selection can be saved as a mask by choosing Save Selection from the Selection menu. When you save a selection, a new grayscale channel is added to the three RGB channels (FIGURE 10:3). The extra grayscale channel is merely a representation of the selection as a mask and does not add any color information to the file. The black and white areas of the mask represent either completely selected or completely deselected parts of the image when the mask is loaded as a selection.

 You can choose whether to have black represent the open part of the mask, which is the default, or if you prefer, white can represent the open mask. Choose your preference from the Channel Options dialog box in the Channels palette (see FIGURE 10:4, *The Channels Palette*).

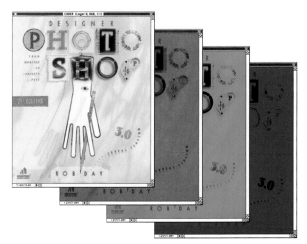

Photoshop's masks are analogous to rubyliths.

FIGURE 10:1

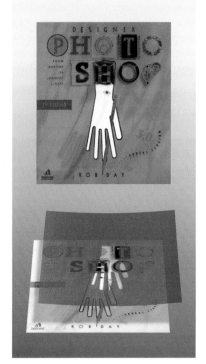

FIGURE 10:2

An RGB Color file is made up of three grayscale channels and a master composite RGB channel for viewing the file's color.

The addition of a new channel increases a file's size. A 3 MB RGB file becomes 4 MB when a channel is added because each of the RGB channels and the new channel are 1 MB, or a third of the original file size. It is wise to use the Photoshop 3.0 format while you work, as the file is automatically compressed when you save it to disk. The compression maintains all of the image detail and the amount of compression depends on the number of repeating pixels. For example, an extra channel with a simple black square on a white background would add almost nothing to a file's size, while an extra channel with a grayscale image in it would make a larger file size (**FIGURE 10:5**).

 An image that has extra channels cannot be saved in EPS, JPEG, or Scitex CT formats. If you want to save a file in one of these formats and save your extra channels, duplicate the file, delete the channels, and choose Save As from the File menu, to save the duplicate file with a new name and format. Or, choose Save a Copy to save a copy of the file in a new format without layers or channels. For more on file formats see Appendix A, *File Formats*.

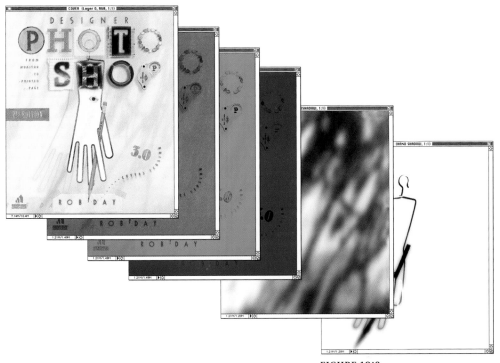

Saved selections are represented by additional grayscale channels.

FIGURE 10:3

The Channels Palette

Choose Show Channels from the Palettes submenu under Window to access the Channels palette (FIGURE A). When you make a selection you can save it to a new channel by choosing Save Selection from the Selection menu. You can also click on the New Selection icon at the bottom of the Channels palette (1) to convert a selection to a mask. Here is an overview of the palette's features:

- **TARGET CHANNEL:** Before you can edit a channel it must be the target layer. Click on the title of the channel you wish to target and its title is highlighted, indicating that it is the target layer (2).
- **EYE ICONS:** Clicking on an Eye icon (3) turns the channel's preview off; clicking again turns it back on. When you preview a mask channel along with

another channel the preview color is determined by the settings in the Channel Option dialog box.

Click on the arrow in the palette's upper right-hand corner to access more Channel options:

- **PALETTE OPTIONS:** Choose Palette Options to select the size of the previews displayed in the palette. Showing the previews in the palette can slow down Photoshop's performance, so turn them off if you can work without them.
- **NEW CHANNEL:** Choose New Channel to add a new blank channel to the document. The Channel Options dialog box appears (FIGURE B) which lets you determine whether the open areas of the mask will be white or black—choosing Selected Areas under Color Indicates means that the open areas of

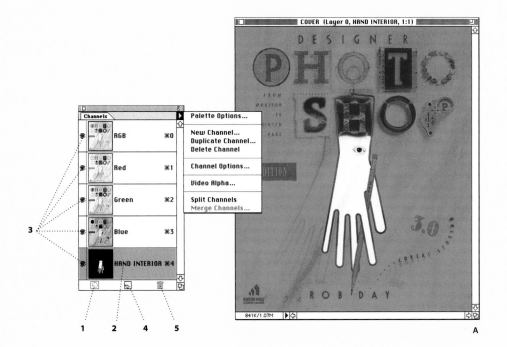

the selection are indicated by black in the channel. The color and opacity of the preview relative to the other previewed channels is determined by adjusting the Opacity value and the patch under Color— click on the patch to get the color picker and choose a color. You can also click the New Channel icon (4) at the bottom of the palette to create a new channel.

• **DUPLICATE CHANNEL:** Choose Duplicate Channel to make a copy of a channel either in the same document or to another document of the same pixel dimensions. Only one channel can be highlighted in the palette for Duplicate Channel to be available. The Duplicate Channel dialog box lets you give the duplicate channel a name and choose where it will be copied. You can choose to copy the channel into

the same document or, if any other documents of the same pixel dimensions are open, by clicking on the Document pop-up menu under Destination. You can also copy the channel as a new document by choosing New. Clicking on the channel's name and Dragging and dropping it on the New Channel icon at the bottom of the palette copies a channel. Or you can drag and drop the name on any document to copy it there.

• **DELETE CHANNEL:** Highlight a mask channel and choose Delete Channel or, click and drag it onto the Trashcan icon (5) at the bottom of the palette to delete a channel.

• **CHANNEL OPTIONS:** Choose Channel Options or double-click a channel name to open the Channel Options dialog. You can rename the mask, choose whether its color indicates a masked or selected area, and alter its preview color and opacity. The opacity setting only effects the preview of a mask channel when it is viewed along with other channels—it has no effect on the actual mask.

• **SPLIT CHANNELS:** Choose Split Channels if you want to separate a multi-channel document in to separate documents.

• **MERGE CHANNELS:** To combine different single-channel documents that have the same pixel dimensions into one document, choose Merge Channels. Three documents can be merged into one RGB or Lab color document or four documents can be merged into one CMYK file.

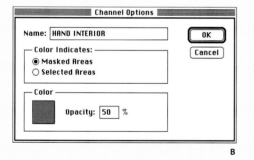

B

When you make a selection only the selected parts of the image can be edited. If you want to work on another part of the image you will have to first deselect—for this reason you may want to save the initial selection so that you can easily reselect the same pixels at a later time. The simplest use of a mask is to save a selection that is made manually, so that it can be reloaded anytime after it has been deselected. However, because masks can add considerable size to a file, using them for this purpose can make a large file unmanageable.

A better way to save a manual selection is to use the Pen tool to make the selection, and then save the pen path. Saving a path does not add any significant size to a file, and there is no limit to the number of paths you can save (Photoshop 3.0 document is limited to 24 total channels). You can also convert a selection made with one of the other selection tools into a path by choosing Make Path from the Paths palette, and then saving the resulting path (see FIGURE 9:9, *The Paths Palette*).

 If you convert a complex selection made by the Magic Wand or Lasso tool to a path and save it, then load the path and convert it back to a selection, the resulting selection may not be identical to the original selection. If you need a selection to be saved perfectly, pixel for pixel, you should save it as a selection, not a path.

Simple masks take up less disk and memory space than complex masks. The mask in Figure A adds 600 K to the 18.8 MB file, while the more complex mask in Figure B adds over 6 MB to the file.

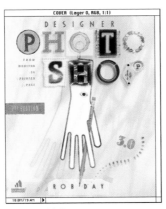
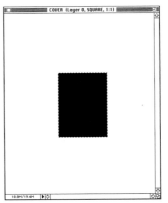

FIGURE 10:5   A   B

The Save Selection dialog lets you determine a Destination for the saved selection.

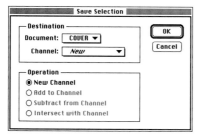

FIGURE 10:6

SAVING A SELECTION   To convert a selection that you have made with one of the selection tools into a mask, you can choose Save Selection from the Select menu, or you can click on the New Selection icon in the lower left corner of the Channels palette. When you choose Save Selection, the Save Selection dialog box appears (**FIGURE 10:6**). This dialog is new with Photoshop 3.0 and lets you determine where and how your selection will be saved.

If there are other documents opened that have the same pixel dimensions as the document with the selection you are saving, you can choose one of those documents from the document pop-up menu under Destination. This lets you choose whether you want to save the selection as a new channel in the document you are working on, or in another open document (**FIGURE 10:7**). If you choose a channel other

FIGURE 10:7

Only documents that have the same pixel dimensions as the active window will show up in Document pop-up menu. In this case HAND SHADOW does not appear in the Document pop-up menu because it is a different size from COVER.

When you save an existing selection it can be added to, subtracted from, or intersected with an existing channel. The target channel can be in another document as long as that document has the same pixel dimensions as the document with the selection. Here the selected area in Figure A is modifying the channel SHADOWS (B). Figures C – E show the results of Add to, Subtract from, and Intersect with Channel.

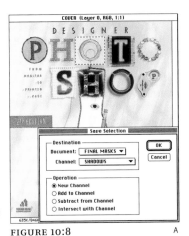

FIGURE 10:8   A

Shadows channel   B

Add to   C

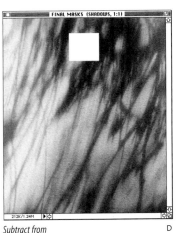

Subtract from   D

Intersect with   E

than New from the Channel pop-up menu, Add to Channel, Subtract from Channel, and Intersect with Channel are available in the Operation menu. Choosing one of these items alters the channel you have chosen from the Channel pop-up menu accordingly (**FIGURE 10:8**).

LOADING A SELECTION   Once you have saved a selection into a channel you will want to load it back as a selection as the need arises. Choose Load Selection from the Selection menu to load a channel as a selection. When you choose Load Selection, the

FIGURE 10:9

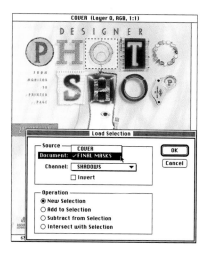

The Load Selection dialog box lets you load a mask channel as a selection. If there are other documents open with the same pixel dimensions as the active window, then their channels as well as the active window's channels can be loaded as selections.

FIGURE 10:10

The Shadow channel loaded as a selection.

Load Selection dialog box appears (**FIGURE 10:9**). If there are other grayscale documents open with the same pixel dimensions as the active window, they will be available in the Source Document pop-up menu. Other color documents with the same pixel dimensions and extra channels will also be available. If there is more than one channel available in the document you can choose a channel from the Channel pop-up menu. Click OK and that channel will be loaded as a selection and the selected pixels can then be edited (**FIGURE 10:10**).

If your document has an active selection when you choose Load Selection, Add to, Subtract from, and Intersect with Selection will be available under Operations in the dialog box. Choosing one of these items will modify your existing selection accordingly as the specified channel is loaded (**FIGURE 10:11**).

If there is an existing selection you can modify it with another mask by choosing Add to, Subtract from, or Intersect with. Figure B shows the active selection intersected with the SHADOWS mask.

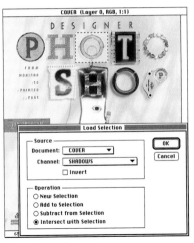

FIGURE 10:11

LOADING SHORTCUTS There are a number of shortcuts for loading saved selections:

- Holding down the Command + Option and typing a channel's number loads that channel.

- You can Option-click the channel's title in the palette to load that channel. If there is an active selection, holding down Option+Shift and clicking a channel's title adds that mask to the current selection. Hold down the Option + Command and click the channel's title to subtract the mask. Holding down the Option+Command+Shift and clicking the channel's number selects the intersection of the two selections.

- You can also click on a channel's title and drag it on to the Selection icon at the bottom of the palette to load it as a selection.

VIEWING AND EDITING CHANNELS Once you have saved selections as channels, you can choose to view and edit the channels in a variety of ways. Each new channel you create is assigned a number. If you are working in RGB mode, the red, green, and blue channels are always numbered 1, 2, and 3, respectively, and the new channels are numbered in order of their creation, starting with the number 4. If want, you can change the order of the mask channels by clicking and dragging them to a new location in the palette.

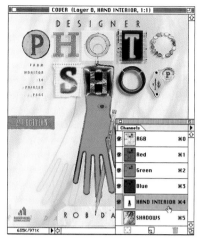

You can choose to pre-view one channel or any combination of channels by clicking the Eye icons on and off in the Channels palette.

FIGURE 10:12

You can view an individual channel in a document by clicking on its title in the Channels palette; or you can type Command plus the channel's number to view that channel. Clicking on the RGB composite channel at the top of the palette brings you back to the color image, or you can type Command+0. If you want to view more than one channel at a time, click in the Channel palette's left column—next to the channel title—to turn its preview on or off. An eye icon indicates the channel is previewing (**FIGURE 10:12**).

You can also decide to edit one or more channels at a time. Only the channels that are highlighted in the palette will be affected as you work. You could decide to edit only the green and blue channels while you preview the full color image by clicking first on the Blue channel, then Shift-clicking on the Green channel, and clicking the eye icon on next to the RGB composite channel (**FIGURE 10:13**).

 If a document has more than one layer, then the background layer must be targeted in the Layers palette in order to edit combinations of channels.

You can choose to edit only two channels by Shift-clicking the two channels' titles in the Channels palette.

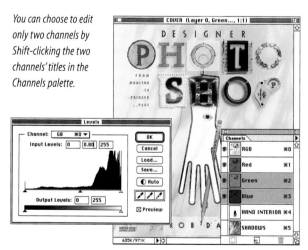

FIGURE 10:13

TEMPORARY MASKS

If there is no need to save a mask, Photoshop's Quick Mask feature lets you create a temporary mask channel (see **FIGURE 10:14**, *Quick Masks*). Quick masks are the same in every respect as a regular mask channel, except that once it is converted into a selection the Quick Mask channel is deleted. With Quick Masks any of the painting tools can be used as selection tools. You might need to make complex selections that have both hard and soft edges and Quick Masks are very

Quick Masks

With Quick Masks you can create a temporary mask without committing it to a channel. You can also work on the mask and see the artwork at the same time—the mask previews as an overlay. This feature makes selecting easier, particularly for beginners. To use Quick Masks:

1 Make a selection and then click once on the right-hand Quick Mask icon in the tool box (FIGURE A). The selection marquee disappears, and all of the nonselected areas are covered with a transparent orange overlay. If you have the Channels palette showing (choose Show Channels from the Window menu), the Quick mask is listed as a new channel titled Mask (FIGURE B). A Quick Mask functions in the same way as a saved selection, except that you can see your artwork as you alter the mask.

2 Double-clicking on the Quick Mask icons displays a dialog box (FIGURE C) that allows you to adjust the transparency and color of the overlay, and to reverse the overlay so that the colored area represents the selected area. Clicking on the color patch in this dialog box displays a Color Picker that allows you to change the overlay color.

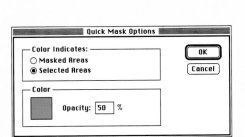

A

B

C

D

3 When the overlay is active, it can be edited with any of the selection and painting tools as if it were a grayscale channel. You can use the selection tools to select an area, then either delete that part of the overlay or fill it with the overlay color. You can also paint on the overlay color. The Color Picker shows grayscale only when a Quick Mask is active. Painting with white removes mask (FIGURE D), black adds mask, and grays add a percentage of mask.

4 Once you have finished editing the overlay, click the left-hand Quick Mask icon and the edited overlay becomes a selection again (FIGURE E).

E

useful for this purpose. I used a Quick Mask, edited with the painting tools, to create the silhouette in FIG-URE 10:15. To make a selection with a Quick Mask:

1 I started the silhouette by creating a path with the Pen tool, which was converted to a selection and then inverted so that the background was selected (FIGURE 10:16).

2 I double-clicked the right-hand Quick Mask icon and set the Color Transparency to 100%, Color Indicates Selected Area in the Quick Mask Options dialog box, and clicked OK (FIGURE 10:17).

3 To make the silhouette believable I wanted its edges to be sharp in some areas and soft in others depending on the focus of the image. Using the Blur Tool with a variety of Pressure percentages and Brush sizes I softened the edges of the mask where the photograph was out of focus (FIGURE 10:18). The blurring had no effect on the actual image because I was only editing the mask.

4 I also used the Airbrush to add or subtract mask in the detail areas, or to touch up the soft edges (FIGURE 10:19). Since I was painting on mask, I could Option-click an area of the image where there was no mask and the painting tool would subtract mask. If I Option-clicked a masked area, the painting tool would again add mask.

FIGURE 10:15

You can create more accurate silhouettes by varying the softness of a mask's edges.

FIGURE 10:16

The Pen tool creates precise hard-edged paths, which can be converted into a selection.

FIGURE 10:17

In this case I chose to have the masked areas of the selection represented by a color with no transparency. I did not want to be confused by the mask preview's transparency as I softened the edges of the mask.

I used the Blur tool to soften the edges that were out of focus.

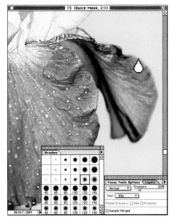

FIGURE 10:18

Painting with black as the foreground color adds mask; painting with white subtracts mask.

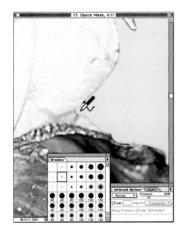

FIGURE 10:19

Converting the Quick Mask to a selection and filling the selection with white reveals the modulated silhouette.

FIGURE 10:20

5 When I was finished editing the Quick Mask I converted it back to a selection by clicking on the left Quick Mask icon. I could then fill the background with white, and any parts of the original selection that I had blurred while it was a mask showed as a soft edge (**FIGURE 10:20**).

 You can also cut a selection made in this manner and paste it in to a new document while maintaining the soft and hard edges of the silhouette. If you select an object on a light colored background, and cut and paste it into a dark background, a light fringe may show on the edges of the selection. In this case you can choose Remove White Matte from the Matting submenu under Select to remove the unwanted light pixels. Choose Remove Black Matte if you are pasting an image cut from a dark background onto a light background (**FIGURE 10:21**).

FIGURE 10:21

If you paste a selection with soft edges, copied from a light background into a dark background, choosing White Matte removes the light fringe from the edges of the floating selection. Choose Black Matte if you are pasting a dark image into a light background.

MASKING TECHNIQUE

A MASK CAN BE BLACK AND WHITE only (the selection is either entirely open or closed when loaded), or it can consist of 256 levels of gray. Having different gray levels in the channel means that when the channel is loaded as a selection, the resulting selection can have areas that are only partially open depending on the gray level. For instance, a 50% gray would produce a selection that is half open and any effects you applied would happen at half strength. Building masks that have different degrees of openness via grayscale channels enables you to create a myriad of special effects.

BLENDS AS MASKS

The simplest use of a channel that is more than just black or white is to create a selection than can be used to apply an effect with varying intensity. This can be accomplished by making a new channel, filling it with a gradient fill from black to white (see **FIGURE 11:1**, *The Gradient Tool*), and loading the channel as a selection. I used this technique to create blended backgrounds for the baseball book jackets (**FIGURE 11:2**) that I illustrated for Creative Education (see Chapter Nine, *The Creative Pixel*). To adjust the color of the background through a gradient mask:

FIGURE 11:1

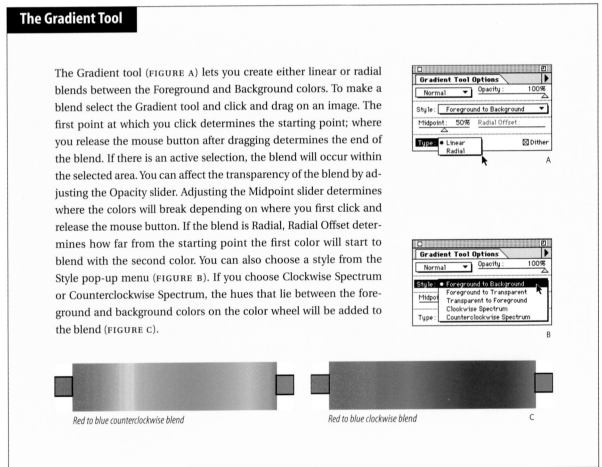

The Gradient Tool

The Gradient tool (FIGURE A) lets you create either linear or radial blends between the Foreground and Background colors. To make a blend select the Gradient tool and click and drag on an image. The first point at which you click determines the starting point; where you release the mouse button after dragging determines the end of the blend. If there is an active selection, the blend will occur within the selected area. You can affect the transparency of the blend by adjusting the Opacity slider. Adjusting the Midpoint slider determines where the colors will break depending on where you first click and release the mouse button. If the blend is Radial, Radial Offset determines how far from the starting point the first color will start to blend with the second color. You can also choose a style from the Style pop-up menu (FIGURE B). If you choose Clockwise Spectrum or Counterclockwise Spectrum, the hues that lie between the foreground and background colors on the color wheel will be added to the blend (FIGURE C).

Red to blue counterclockwise blend

Red to blue clockwise blend

FIGURE 11:2

1 I started by selecting the player with the Pen tool and saving the resulting path. I then converted the grayscale image into a textured bitmap as described in Chapter Nine, FIGURES 9:30 – 9:36.

2 Next, I created a new channel by clicking the New Channel icon in the Channels palette. With the foreground and background colors set to black and white, respectively, I double-clicked on the Gradient tool to open the Gradient Tool Options palette. I specified a Linear Blend, with a Midpoint Skew of 50% and a style of Normal. I also checked the Dither box in the lower right-hand corner to help prevent banding from occurring in the blend (**FIGURE 11:3**).

The Gradient Options palette set to a Linear Blend with a Midpoint Skew of 50%. Checking the Dither box adds noise to the blend to prevent banding.

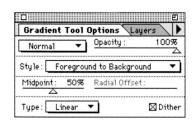

FIGURE 11:3

3 Starting from the top of the image, I clicked and dragged the cursor to the bottom, creating a blend from black at the top, to white at the bottom (**FIGURE 11:4**). The percentage that I specified as the Midpoint Skew determined where the blend would break—where a blend breaks can also be altered by using Levels. Open Levels and move the middle Input slider left or right, and you can adjust the break interactively (**FIGURE 11:5**).

4 Because I did not want the player selected when the blend mask was loaded as a selection, I converted the silhouette I had made with the Pen tool into a selection, and filled the selection with white. In this case I had specified Color Indicates Selected Area in the Channel

Clicking and dragging on the image with the Gradient tool makes a blend of the Foreground and Background colors.

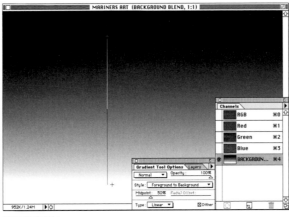

FIGURE 11:4

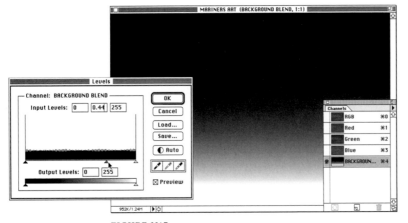

Rather than adjusting the Gradient Options and remaking the blend, you can use Levels to adjust where a blend breaks by moving the middle Input slider.

FIGURE 11:5

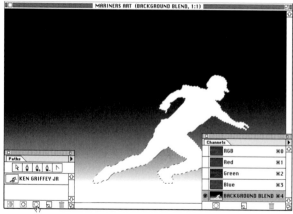

FIGURE 11:6

The Pen path defining the player's silhouette was loaded and filled with white in the blend channel.

Options dialog, so white areas of the mask would not be selected when the mask was loaded (**FIGURE 11:6**)

5 With the blend completed, I returned to the RGB preview (Command + 0) and Option-clicked the blend channel's title in the palette; this loaded the blend mask as a selection (**FIGURE 11:7**).

6 Finally, I opened Hue/Saturation (Command + U) and adjusted the Hue, Saturation, and Lightness sliders until I had the desired blend (**FIGURE 11:8**).

When you load a mask that has grayscale elements, any operation that you perform is modified by the values of the mask's pixels. In this case, I adjusted the hue, saturation, and lightness of the background, and because the blended mask was loaded, any adjustments occurred gradually relative to the gray val-

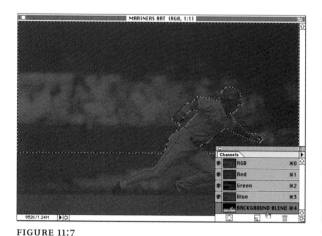

FIGURE 11:7

The selection marquee for the loaded grayscale mask.

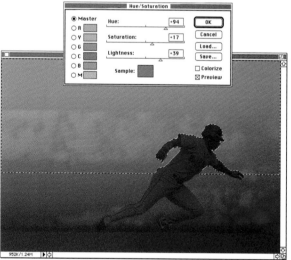

FIGURE 11:8

The color correction was applied with varying strength, depending on the mask's gray level.

ues in the blend. The background was adjusted the most at the top, where the mask was solid black, and was not adjusted at all at the bottom, where the mask was solid white. In the middle of the blend, where the mask is a 50% gray value, the color changed half as much.

 Unless otherwise noted, the examples in this chapter use the default Channel Options setting which is: Color Indicates Selected Area.

FADE OUTS USING BLENDED MASKS You can also use a blend mask to fade away parts of an image. I made the diver in FIGURE 11:9 gradually fade to white with the following method:

1 I silhouetted the diver and then clicked on the New Channel icon at the bottom of the palette, chose Color Indicates Selected Area, an Opacity of 100%, and clicked OK (FIGURE 11:10).

2 In this case I wanted to see the mask in relationship to the image as I edited it, so I targeted the channel by clicking on its title in the palette, and clicked on the Eye icon to the left of the RGB composite channel (FIGURE 11:11). Because I had specified the mask's preview to be an Opacity of 100%, it would show exactly how the blend in the mask broke in relationship to the image.

FIGURE 11:9

The new channel was set to Color Indicates Selected Area, with the preview color at 100% Opacity.

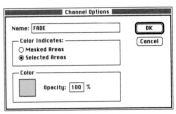

FIGURE 11:10

3 I created the blend in the new channel, and I could see it along with the diver, because all the Eye icons were clicked on. When you view more than one channel at a time, the mask channels preview as the color you specified in the Channel Options dialog box (**FIGURE 11:12**).

4 Previewing the mask and image together let me position the blend mask accurately. I could use Levels to change the break of the blend (FIGURE

11:4) or I could set the background color to black, and use the Move tool to change the position of the blend (**FIGURE 11:13**).

5 After positioning the blend, I clicked the channel's Eye icon off, Option-clicked the channels title in the palette, targeted the RGB composite channel, and filled the resulting selection with white (**FIGURE 11:14**).

Clicking both the mask and RGB composite channel's Eye icons on lets you view the image and mask simultaneously.

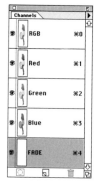

FIGURE 11:11

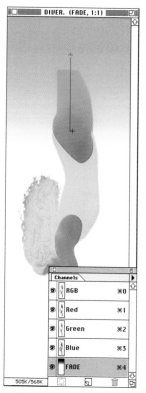

FIGURE 11:12

With the FADE channel targeted and all of the channel's eye icons turned on, I could make the blend in the FADE channel and view it in relationship to the RGB image.

FIGURE 11:13

Using the Move tool with the Background color set to black, I could easily adjust the blend in relationship to the image.

FILTERS THROUGH MASKS The way a filter is applied to an image can by modified by applying it through a mask. I built another blend mask for the diver, which I used to selectively distort the image. In this case I chose Color Indicates Masked Area from the Channel Options dialog because I wanted to see the area of the image that would be distorted by the filter when I previewed the mask and image together (**FIGURE 11:15**).

I converted the new mask to a selection, chose the ZigZag filter from the Distort submenu under Filter, set the style to Pond ripples, Amount to –12, Ridges to 10, and clicked OK (**FIGURE 11:16**). Because the blend channel was loaded as a selection, the ZigZag filter was applied with varying intensity depending on the gray level of the mask. Any filter can be applied through a mask. **FIGURE 11:17** shows some other filters run through this mask.

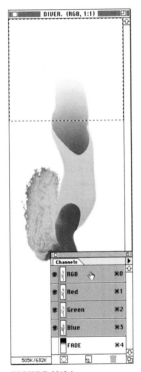

FIGURE 11:14

Once the blend was in the desired position, I loaded it as a selection and filled with white.

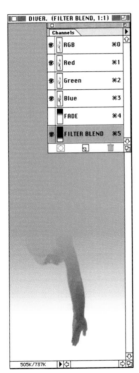

FIGURE 11:15

I made another blend mask, but this time chose Color Indicates Masked Area as the preview for the mask; in this case the preview showed the parts of the image that would be selected.

FIGURE 11:16

The Zig Zag filter applied through the blend mask.

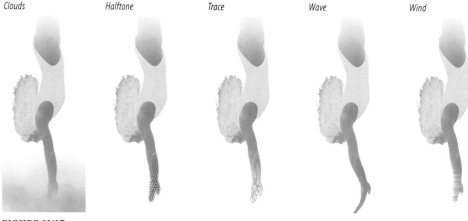

Clouds　　Halftone　　Trace　　Wave　　Wind

FIGURE 11:17

Any filter can be applied through a mask.

FIGURE 11:18

FIGURE 11:19

GRAYSCALE MASKS

Masks can be more complex than simple blends and black and white selections. Any grayscale image can be used as a mask, which can be very useful for coloring grayscale images. Though it is very easy to colorize any grayscale image using the color-correcting tools, I find that with masks I can make more specific color choices and I generally have more control over the image. I used grayscale masks to create the S in Photoshop for *Designer Photoshop's* cover illustration (**FIGURE 11:18**). To make grayscale masks:

1 I started by scanning a torn scrap of note book paper and a slide of clouds (**FIGURE 11:19**).

2 The S was created using 3 masks. I made the first

mask by adding a new channel, which I titled S, and using the Type tool to set an uppercase S filled with black in the channel (**FIGURE 11:20**). See **FIGURE 11:21**, *The Type Tool.*

3 I duplicated the S mask by clicking and dragging its title in the Channels palette onto the New Channel icon. I double-clicked on the copied channel's title and renamed it S Blurred and clicked OK. I blurred the copied S by choosing Gaussian Blur from the Blur submenu under Filter and setting a Radius of 15 (**FIGURE 11:22**).

An uppercase S was set in a new channel and filled with black on a white background.

FIGURE 11:20

The Type Tool

Because Photoshop is a bitmap program and not object-oriented, setting much more than a few words of type with any precision can be very cumbersome. For complex typography you should set the type in another program, such as Illustrator, and import it into Photoshop (see **FIGURES 13:14–13:21**). If the typesetting is not complex, use Photoshop's Type tool, and set the type as follows in an extra channel or layer:

1 Set the Foreground and Background colors to the default black and white (pressing the D key is a shortcut for setting the default colors). Click once on the right-hand Quick Mask icon and select the Type tool (pressing the Y key is a shortcut for selecting the Type tool).

2 Click once in the document's window and the Type Tool dialog box appears (**FIGURE A**). Type the text in the text box at the bottom of the dialog box. You can then choose Font, Size, Leading, Spacing, and Align-

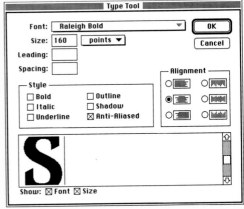

A

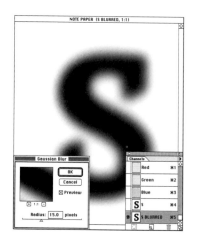

A duplicate of the S channel was blurred.

FIGURE 11:22

FIGURE 11:21

ment specifications for the type. The type will be aligned based on where you clicked inside the window. Check the Anti-Aliased box if you want smooth-edged type. If you are setting small, black type on a light colored background leave Anti-Aliased unchecked; in this case you will need a higher resolution (see FIGURE 5:4).

3 Click OK, and the type will appear in the Quick Mask (FIGURE B). With the type set in a Quick Mask, you can alter the spacing by selecting the letters using the Rectangular Marquee and pressing the arrow keys. The arrow keys will move the selected area in 1 pixel increments or, if the Shift key is pressed, in 10 pixel increments.

4 When you are satisfied with the type's position, click the left-hand Quick Mask icon to convert the type into a selection and fill with a color or adjust the type with one of the color correction tools (FIGURE C).

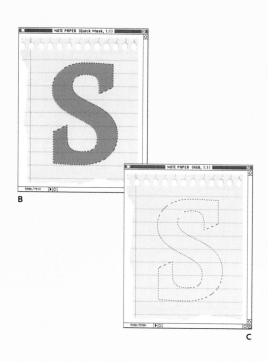

4 I made the third mask by adding another new channel, pasting the cloud scan into that channel, loading the S channel as a selection by Option-clicking its title in the Channels palette, inverting the selection by choosing Inverse from the Select menu, and filling the resulting selection with white. I named this channel Clouds (**FIGURE 11:23**).

5 Now I could use the three masks to color the S. I clicked on the RGB channel (Command+0), loaded the S Blurred mask, and filled the selection with a pale green (**FIGURE 11:24**).

6 Next, I loaded the S mask and used Levels to lighten the green (**FIGURE 11:25**).

7 Finally, I Loaded the Cloud mask and filled it with dark blue (**FIGURE 11:26**). At this point I could also reload any of the masks and further adjust the color and contrast of the S.

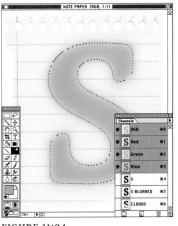

FIGURE 11:23

Clouds were pasted into a third channel, the S BLURRED channel was loaded, the selection was inverted, and filled with white.

FIGURE 11:24

The S BLURRED channel was loaded and filled with a pale green.

The S channel was loaded as a selection, and the paper was lightened using Levels.

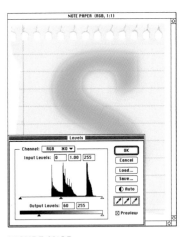

FIGURE 11:25

FIGURE 11:26

The CLOUDS mask was loaded and filled with dark blue.

FIGURE 11:27

PAINTING THROUGH A MASK

A grayscale mask can also be used as painting guide. Etienne Delessert used three masks created from a scanned painting to create the Photoshop piece shown in **FIGURE 11:27**. Eteinne is a world-renowned editorial and children's book illustrator. His work can often be seen in *The New York Times*, as well as the *Atlantic Monthly* and other magazines. His work has hung in galleries throughout the world, including a one-man show at the Louvre's Museum of Decorative Arts. He was born in Lausanne, Switzerland, and lives in Lakeville, Connecticut.

BUILDING THE MASKS Etienne started by scanning a snapshot that he had taken at a gallery in Bologne, Italy, where he was having a one-man show. He also scanned a reproduction of two large, abstract heads that he had painted, which he would use to make the masks (**FIGURE 11:28**). To make the masks:

1 Etienne started by adding a new channel to the scan of the Bologne gallery, which he named Black Heads. With both the RGB and new channels previewing, he cut and pasted the scan of

FIGURE 11:28

the heads into the Black Heads channel. He could then scale and position them relative to the gallery scan (**FIGURE 11:29**).

2 Next he double-clicked the Magic Wand tool, set its Tolerance to 50 with Anti-aliased checked in the Magic Wand Options palette, clicked on the Black Heads title in the Channels palette, and clicked on the background of the Black Heads channel (**FIGURE 11:30**).

3 He inverted the resulting selection and saved it as a new mask by clicking on the Selection icon in the lower right-hand corner of the palette. He named the new channel Head Silhouette (**FIGURE 11:31**).

4 Etienne duplicated the Black Heads channel by clicking and dragging its title into the New Channel icon at the bottom of the palette. He named this new channel White Head and then loaded Head Silhouette by Option-clicking its title. He

The scans of the paintings were pasted into a new channel viewed here with both the channel and composite RGB previews turned on.

FIGURE 11:29

Etienne selected the background of the BLACK HEADS channel with the Magic Wand.

FIGURE 11:30

The HEAD SILHOUETTE mask.

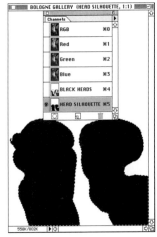

FIGURE 11:31

The WHITE HEAD channel made by loading HEAD SILHOUETTE and inverting the selected pixels.

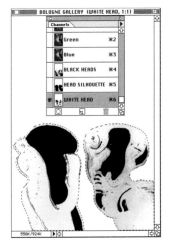

FIGURE 11:32

The HEAD SILHOUETTE mask loaded as a selection into the RGB image and filled with white.

FIGURE 11:33

The BLACK HEADS mask loaded as a selection and filled with black.

FIGURE 11:34

FIGURE 11:35

then chose Invert from the Map submenu under Image to finish the third mask (**FIGURE 11:32**). Note that Invert is different from Inverse found under Selection; Invert makes a negative of the selected pixels.

Etienne could now use the three masks to selectively paint the heads into the gallery scan:

1 First he loaded Head Silhouette as a selection and filled the selection with white (**FIGURE 11:33**).

2 Next he loaded the Black Head mask and filled it with black (**FIGURE 11:34**).

3 With the Black Head mask loaded, Etienne could add color with the painting tools and only the black areas of the heads would be affected. He could also paint the white areas of the head, by loading the White Head mask, without affecting the black areas or the background (**FIGURE 11:35**).

Etienne colored the heads by loading the masks and applying color through the masks with the Paintbrush and Smudge tool.

MAKING PHOTOSHOP PAGE GUIDES

Photoshop does not officially have the capability of showing page guides the way most page layout and drawing programs do; however, you can create guides using the Line tool and an extra channel. To make page guides:

1 Open the Channels palette and click the New Channel icon. Name the new channel Guides in the Channel Options dialog box. Choose Color Indicates Selected Area—you can also choose a color for previewing the guide mask (**FIGURE 11:36**). Click OK. The new channel should be filled with white.

2 Click the Eye icons for both the Guide channel and the color composite channel on, and target the Guide channel in the Channels palette (**FIGURE 11:37**).

3 Double-click the Line tool and set the mode to Normal, Opacity to 100%, Line Width 1 or 2 pixels, and uncheck the anti-aliased box (**FIGURE 11:38**).

4 With the Foreground color set to black, draw out any guide lines that you might need. Hold down the Shift key to constrain the line to the nearest 45° angle. Open the Info palette and you can start the lines at a precise x or y coordinate. As you work simply click the Guide mask's Eye icon on to view the guides with your image, or off to hide the guides (**FIGURE 11:39**). The guide mask will add little to the file size as it is only black and white.

An extra channel can be used to show page guides in Photoshop documents.

FIGURE 11:36

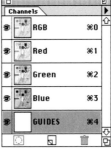

Target the GUIDES channel, and view it with the RGB composite channel.

FIGURE 11:37

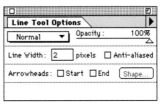

Set the Line width to 1 or 2 pixels with Anti-aliased unchecked.

FIGURE 11:38

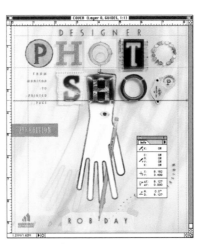

With the Line tool selected, press Shift, and click and drag out the guide lines.

FIGURE 11:39

STORING MASKS

Photoshop has a limit of 24 channels per document, but it is possible to store extra masks in other documents, and load them from those documents. This feature is also useful when you are trying to limit the file size of an image. You can copy masks into a separate document, save the new file, and then delete the masks from the original file. To archive your masks:

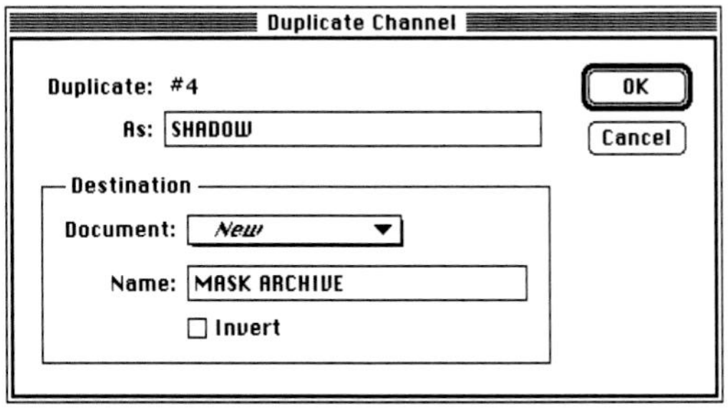

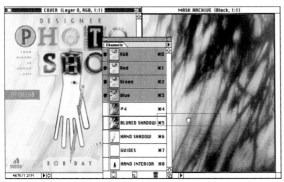

FIGURE 11:40

Duplicate Channel lets you copy a channel to a new document.

FIGURE 11:41

A new feature of Photoshop 3.0 allows you to drag and drop channels from one document to another.

1 Open the Channels palette and click on the title of the first mask channel in your document. Choose Duplicate Channel and choose New from the Destination pop-up menu and type a name in the Name field. Click OK and the channel is copied to a new file with the title you specified (**FIGURE 11:40**).

2 Click on the window of the original document. Click and drag the title of the second mask channel and drop it on the copy of the first channel; this makes a copy of the second channel into the duplicate file, which becomes a two-channel document (**FIGURE 11:41**).

3 Repeat step 2 for any other channels you want to move into the new document. Save the new document and delete the channels from the original file.

4 You can now close the mask archive and continue to work. If you want to load one of the archived masks; open the archive, click on the original file and choose Load Selection. Choose the mask archive's title from the Document pop-up menu, and the channel you want to load from the Channel pop-up menu, and click OK. The specified channel is loaded. You can close the mask archive and continue to work.

LAYERS

PHOTOSHOP LETS YOU TREAT THE parts of a composited image as discreet objects, which can be moved and edited at will. The Layers palette gives you the freedom to assign floating selections to separate layers without altering the pixels beneath the selection. Layers are analogous to having parts of your image on clear pieces of film stacked on top of each other (**FIGURE 12:1**). The option to add layers to a document does not come without a price—extra layers add to a file's size. How much a file will grow depends on the amount of transparency in the added layers. A new layer is transparent until you paste or paint pixels into it. The transparent areas add nothing to the file size, so a multi-layered document with small objects in each layer might have a smaller file size than a two-layered document where both layers have little or no transparent areas.

FIGURE 12:1

A document's layers are analogous to having images pasted on to clear film and then stacking the films on top of each other.

ADDING LAYERS

A layered file can only be saved in Photoshop 3.0 format. If you choose Save As from the file menu only the Photoshop 3.0 format will be available. When you choose Save a Copy, other formats will be available, but if you choose another format, any layers or channels will be discarded from the copied document. Save a Copy allows you to save a copy of the file in its current state, while you continue to work on the original file. If you choose Save As, the file is saved as it is, and you continue to work on that file.

To add a new layer to a document, show the Layers palette by choosing Show Layers from the Palette submenu under Window (see **FIGURE 12:2**, *The Layers Palette*). Click on the arrow in the upper right-hand corner of the palette and choose New Layer from the pop-up menu, or click the New Layer icon at the bottom of the palette. The New Layer dialog box lets you name the layer and assign it attributes

You can organize layers, create new layers, and apply different attributes to existing layers in a document via the Layers palette. Choose Show Layers from the Palettes submenu under Window to show the Layers palette (FIGURE A). Here is an overview of the palette's features:

- **TARGET LAYER:** Before you can edit a layer it must be the target layer. Click on the title of the layer you wish to target and its title is highlighted, indicating that it is the target layer (1). The targeted layer's title also appears in the document's title bar.

- **EYE ICONS:** Clicking on an Eye icon (2) turns the layer's preview off, clicking again turns it back on. Option-clicking an Eye icon makes only that layer visible, while option clicking again turns on all of the layers' previews.

- **MOVE ICONS:** Click on the column to the right of the Eye icons to link another layer to the targeted layer (3). In this case you can click and drag to move the objects in the linked layers simultaneously, if there are no selections, and the Move tool is selected in the tool box.

- **PRESERVE TRANSPARENCY:** Check the Preserve Transparency (4) to mask the transparent areas of the targeted layer from any edits.

- **CLIPPING GROUPS:** A Clipping Group is indicated by dotted lines between the group's layers. The title of the base layer in the group is underlined (5). See page 169 for more on Clipping Groups.

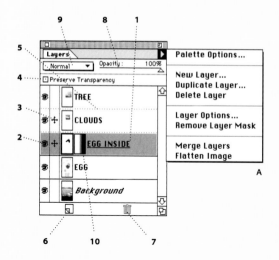

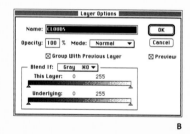

Click on the arrow in the upper right corner of the palette to access the palette's pop-up menu:

- **PALETTE OPTIONS:** Choose Palette Options to change the size of the preview icons that appear in the palette. Turning off the previews by choosing None can improve the performance of Photoshop.

- **NEW LAYER:** Choose New Layer or click on the New layer icon (6) to add a new layer. The New Layer dialog box lets you assign attributes to the layer. Option-clicking the New Layer icon bypasses the New Layer dialog box and a layer with default attributes is created.

- **DUPLICATE LAYER:** Choose Duplicate Layer to make a copy of a targeted layer to the same or another document. You can also copy a layer from one document to another by clicking and dragging its title from the palette into the window of the other document.

- **DELETE LAYER:** Target a layer and choose Delete Layer or drag the layer's title into the Trash icon (7) to remove a layer and its objects from the document.

- **LAYER OPTIONS:** Choose Layer options to change the Opacity or Mode of an existing layer. You can also adjust a layer's opacity by moving the palette's Opacity slider (8), or its mode by clicking on the Mode pop-up menu (9). The Layer Options dialog box also lets you blend the layer's pixels with the underlying pixels. For example, moving the left-hand slider under This Layer blends the layer's shadows with the underlying pixels; moving the right-hand slider blends the layer's highlights (FIGURE B). By holding down the Option key and clicking and dragging on the triangles, you can split the triangles and soften the blending.

- **ADD LAYER MASK:** You can add a mask to a layer (10) by choosing Add Layer Mask (see page 163 for more on Layer Masks). If there is an existing Layer Mask, this menu item reads Remove Layer Mask. When you choose Remove Layer Mask, you have the option to permanently apply the mask or discard it.

- **MERGE LAYERS:** If you want to merge two or more layers without flattening the image, turn on the Eye icons of only the layers you want to merge, and choose Merge Layers. One of the previewed layers must be targeted for Merge Layers to be available.

- **FLATTEN IMAGE:** When you have finished working on an image choose Flatten Image to merge all of the layers. Images must be flattened before they can be saved in a format other than Photoshop 3.0.

(**FIGURE 12:3**). How the objects pasted into a layer interact with the layers below it is determined by the layer's Opacity and Mode settings. Enter a percentage in the Opacity box to make the layer and any object pasted into that layer transparent and choose a color mode from the Mode pop-up menu to determine how the pixels' colors will blend with the layers below

Name and assign attributes to a new layer in the New Layer dialog box.

FIGURE 12:3

Neutral Layer Fills

When you choose New Layer from the Layers palette, the layer you create is completely transparent until you paste an object into, or paint on, the layer. If you make or load a selection, the color correction tools will not work unless you first fill the selection with a color. For example, if you wanted to create a shadow on a background, you could build a mask, load it as a selection, open Levels, and move the white Output slider to the left, adjusting the pixels of the background to make the shadow. If you load the same mask into a targeted layer that is transparent, then none of

the color correction tools will work because there are no existing pixels to adjust (FIGURE A).

You can choose to fill a new layer with a neutral color that will appear transparent depending on the mode (this option is not available with Normal, Dissolve, Hue, Saturation, Color, or Luminosity). For example, if you choose Multiply from the Mode menu, you can check Fill with Multiply-neutral color (white) and the new layer will be filled with white pixels. The white fill will appear transparent to the layers below because of the Multiply mode. You can now load a mask and use any of the color correction tools (FIGURE B).

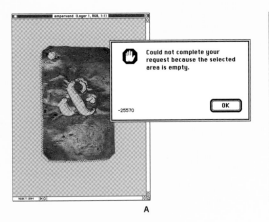

A

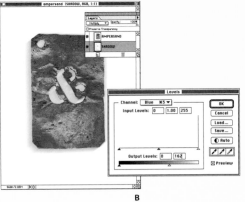

B

(see FIGURE 9:38, *Color Modes*). You can also choose to include the new layer in a clipping group by checking Group With Previous Layer (see page 169 for more on clipping groups). If you are assigning a Mode other than Normal, Dissolve, Hue, Saturation, Color, or Luminosity, you can choose to fill the new layer with a neutral pixel color (see FIGURE 12:4, *Neutral Layer Fills*). Click OK and and the new layer is added to the Layers palette—you now have a two-layered document consisting of a Background and the new layer.

 When viewed alone, the transparent areas of a layer appear as a checkerboard pattern; this lets you distinguish between white pixels and transparent areas when you view one layer at a time. You can alter the way the pattern appears by choosing Transparency from the Preferences submenu (**FIGURE 12:5**).

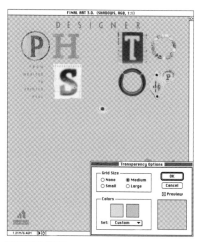

FIGURE 12:5

You can alter the way transparent areas of a Layer preview by choosing Transparency from the Preferences file.

TARGETING A LAYER   An important concept to grasp when learning about layers is targeting. When you make a multi-layered document you can edit only one layer at a time, so it is important to be aware of which layer is the target, or active layer. The target layer's title is highlighted in the Layers palette and any adjustments you make to the file will occur only in that layer. To target another layer simply click on its title. There are shortcuts for targeting a layer. Press Command +] to target the layer above the currently targeted layer; press Command + [to target the next layer down. Press Option + Command +] to target the top layer; Option + Command + [targets the bottom layer. When you edit a layer the attributes assigned to it influence the adjustments you make. For example, if the layer's Opacity is set to 50%, then no element can be more opaque than 50%. If you fill a selection with 100% of a color it will appear as 50%.

 When you target a layer it is important to note that you can also target an individual channel in the Channels palette at the same time. If an extra channel mask is targeted in the Channels palette, then only that channel, not the targeted layer, will be affected as you work. If a channel mask is targeted in the Channels palette, then the highlight color of the targeted layer in the Layers palette is a lighter shade of gray and the preview icon does not have a black border (FIGURE 12:6).

FLOATING SELECTIONS AND LAYERS When you paste an object onto a background or layer, it appears as a floating selection. If you deselect the floating selection it is permanently pasted into the background, or into the layer you have targeted. Deselecting the floating selection discards the original pixels of the layer and replaces them with the floating selection's pixels. If you do not want to destroy the underlying pixels, the floating selection can be made into a new layer. A floating selection can be made into a new layer in three different ways: Choose Make Layer from the palette's pop-up menu, double-click Floating Selection in the palette, or click the New Layer icon at the bottom of the palette. Any of these moves opens the New Layer dialog box, which lets you save the floating selection as a new layer.

 If a floating selection is converted into a layer you cannot apply a mode-neutral color to the layer. To apply a neutral color you must first make the new layer, then paste the object into that layer (see **FIGURE 12:4**, *Neutral Layer Fills*).

It is very easy to inadvertently deselect a floating selection and paste it into a layer, so it is always wise to assign a floating selection to a new layer until you are sure of where it should be and how it will blend with the layers below. Once you are sure of the object's position and attributes it can be merged with any layer or background. Click on the Eye icons for the layers you want to merge (only those layers should be visible), target one of the layers to be merged, and choose Merge Layers from the palette pop-up menu (**FIGURE 12:7**).

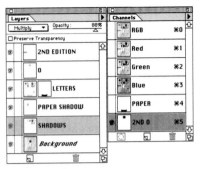

FIGURE 12:6

A targeted layer's title is a lighter shade of gray in the Layers palette if an extra channel mask is the target in the Channels palette.

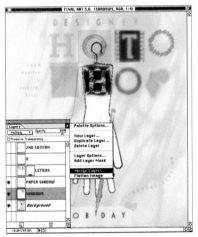

FIGURE 12:7

To merge two or more layers, click on their Eye icons in the Layers palette to make them the only visible layers, and choose Merge Layers from the palette menu.

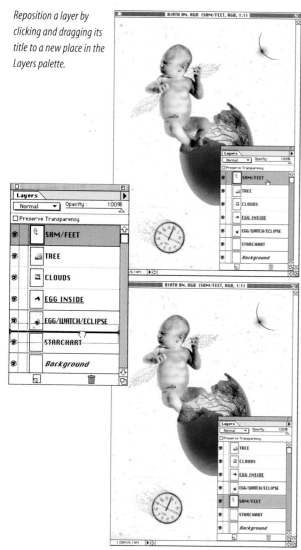

FIGURE 12:8

EDITING LAYERS

As you add layers to a document there are other layer-related tools which add flexibility to the way you organize and edit the document's layers. Using Layer Masks and Clipping Groups gives you the equivalent of unlimited undos for many Photoshop functions. Layers add a new dimension to the flexibility of Photoshop, but it also adds to the program's complexity, so it is important to learn how to manage a document's layers.

REORDERING LAYERS If you wish to change the order of a document's layers, simply click and drag on the layer's title in the palette and drop it above the title of the channel you wish to have it appear over (**FIGURE 12:8**). You cannot move the Background layer in this manner unless you convert it to a layer. You can convert the background to a layer by double-clicking Background in the palette to get the Make Layer dialog box. The Background layer is converted to Layer 0 when you click OK. You can now change its sequence in the palette.

PRESERVE TRANSPARENCY When you use the painting tools on a layer with transparent areas, you can paint over both the transparent areas and any objects in the layer. I used Preserve Transparency to color-correct the stones forming the second O in Photoshop on *Designer Photoshop's* cover. To paint color on the stones using the Airbrushes' Color Only mode, I could zoom in and painstakingly color within the edges of each stone, or I could attempt to select the stones, masking off the rest of the image before applying color. The easiest solution is to target the layer that the stones are on and check the Preserve Transparency box at the top of the Layers palette. This ensures that the transparent areas of the layer remain transparent while editing the layer (**FIGURE 12:9**). Typing the / key is a shortcut for toggling Preserve Transparency on and off.

 There is a way of quickly selecting the nontransparent areas of a layer, which accomplishes the same effect as Preserve Transparency—pressing Command+Option+T selects everything but the transparent areas of the targeted layer.

SAMPLE MERGED   Some tools depend on existing pixels in order to work—the Magic Wand, Paint Bucket, Rubber Stamp, Smudge, and Focus tools all work relative to the pixels clicked on. You can decide whether you want these tools to affect only the pixels on the targeted layer or the pixels in all of the layers simultaneously. For example, if you want to blur the edges of an object without also blurring its background, you can double-click the Blur tool and make sure Sample Merged in the Focus Tool Options palette is unchecked. This protects the background from also being blurred. Checking Sample Merged allows you to apply the blur to all the layers of the image (**FIGURE 12:10**).

Checking Sample Merged in the Focus Tool Options palette causes all of the layers to be affected by the Blur tool (A). Unchecking the box protects layers other than the targeted one from being blurred (B).

A

FIGURE 12:10

B

You can paint on the transparent areas of a layer, but if you check Preserve Transparency in the Layers palette, the transparent areas will be masked.

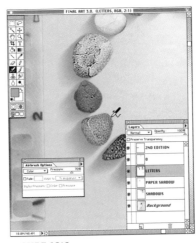

FIGURE 12:9

When a layer is targeted, its Layer mask appears in the Channels palette.

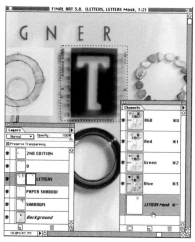

FIGURE 12:11

The Layer Mask Options dialog box.

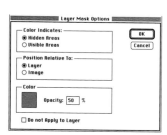

FIGURE 12:12

LAYER MASKS

You can add an additional Layer Mask to each layer you create in a document. This powerful feature makes it possible to have more than one degree of transparency in a given layer. A Layer Mask also makes it possible to have the equivalent of unlimited undos for many of the operations you might perform on the layer. A Layer mask is an extra grayscale channel which allows you to add to, or take away, any degree of transparency from the objects in the targeted layer. The mask only affects the preview of the target layer, so you can add or subtract from the Layer Mask at will without actually altering the pixels in the layer. Once you finish editing a Layer Mask, you can choose to apply the mask to the target layer (altering the layer's pixels), or you can discard the mask, leaving the target layer untouched.

ADDING A LAYER MASK To add a Layer Mask, target a layer and choose Add Layer Mask from the Layers palette menu. If you have turned on the palette's preview icons via the Palette Options dialog, a second preview icon will appear to the right of the targeted layer preview icon, which is a preview of the Layer Mask. A layer's Layer Mask also appears in the Channels palette when that layer is targeted. You can click the Layer Mask's Eye icon on in the Channels palette to view the contents of the Mask by itself or as an overlay on the image (**FIGURE 12:11**).

If you double-click the Layer Mask's preview, the Layer Mask Options dialog box opens (**FIGURE 12:12**). You can choose whether the color will hide or reveal the layer beneath the mask. Color Indicates Hidden Areas is the default. In this case if you paint black in the mask it will completely hide the layer below. Any gray values you paint will make the layer more or less transparent depending on the value. You also can choose to have the Layer Mask move with the underlying layer if you move that layer with the Move tool. Under Position Relative To: choosing Image always keeps the mask stationary, choosing Layer moves the mask with the layer.

 To move a layer and its mask together you must target the layer and use the Move tool while there are no active selections in the document. If you select an object in the layer and move it, the Layer Mask remains stationary.

If you want to temporarily hide the effects of the mask from the targeted layer without actually discarding the mask, check Do Not Apply to Layer. In this case a red X will appear over the Layer Mask's preview in the palette. You can also click on the Layer Mask's palette preview icon with the Command key pressed to temporarily hide its effects. Clicking the preview again with the Command key pressed toggles the mask back on (**FIGURE 12:13**).

USING LAYER MASKS   There are many uses for a Layer Mask. The most obvious is to add or subtract part of an object within a Layer using the painting tools. With a Layer Mask you can delete part of an object in one work session, then reopen the file the next day and add any part of the deleted object back to the image. In Chapter Ten I described how to create a silhouette that has different degrees of sharp-

To disable a Layer Mask without discarding it, press the Command key and click on the Layer Mask's preview icon in the palette.

FIGURE 12:13

FIGURE 12:14

Paste the object to be silhouetted into a new layer.

Make the initial silhouette with the Pen tool, save the path, and add a Layer Mask to the layer.

FIGURE 12:15

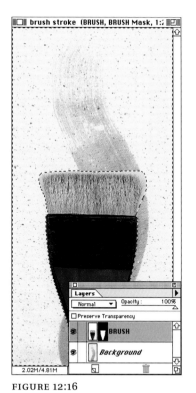

Convert the path to a selection, invert the resulting selection, target the Layer Mask, and fill with black to hide the selected area.

FIGURE 12:16

ness along its edges using a Quick Mask. If the silhouetted object is to appear on top of another image, then making the silhouette with a Layer Mask gives you more flexibility editing the silhouette. To make a silhouette using a Layer Mask:

1 Paste the object to be silhouetted onto the background document and double-click Floating Selection in the palette to convert it to a new layer (**FIGURE 12:14**).

2 Make an initial selection of the silhouette using the Pen tool and save the path. Target the new layer and choose Add Layer Mask from the Layers palette (**FIGURE 12:15**).

3 Target the Layer Mask by clicking on its preview icon in the palette. Convert the saved silhouette path to a selection and invert the selection. Your color picker will be grayscale, because you have targeted the grayscale Layer Mask. With the Foreground color 100% black, press Option+Delete; this fills the selected area in the Layer Mask with black and hides the corresponding areas of the layer (**FIGURE 12:16**).

Edit the edges of the Layer Mask with the Painting and Focus tools.

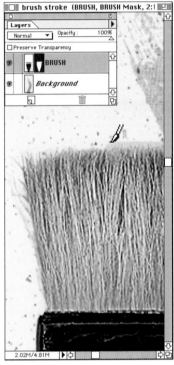

FIGURE 12:17

Make a selection around the object to be made transparent.

FIGURE 12:18

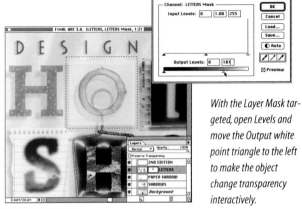

FIGURE 12:19

With the Layer Mask targeted, open Levels and move the Output white point triangle to the left to make the object change transparency interactively.

4 You can now target the Layer Mask and edit the silhouette with the painting tools as was described in Chapter Ten (see FIGURES 10:18–10:20). Painting with black hides the image in the layer, painting with white reveals the image (FIGURE 12:17).

VARYING TRANSPARENCY WITHIN A LAYER
You can also use a Layer Mask to vary the transparency of different objects within the layer. This is useful when you have separate objects in one layer. When you add a Layer to a document its opacity is determined in the Layer Options dialog box, or by adjusting the Opacity slider in the palette when the layer is

targeted. Any objects pasted into a layer assume the opacity of that layer. If you want to adjust the opacity of each object separately, you must either create new layers for each object, or leave the Opacity at 100% and modulate the transparency with a Layer Mask. To change transparency with a Layer Mask:

1 Target the Layer with the objects and choose Add Layer Mask from the palette.

2 With the Rectangular or Ellipse selection tool, draw a selection around an object that is to be made transparent (FIGURE 12:18).

3 Target the Layer Mask and open Levels. Move the

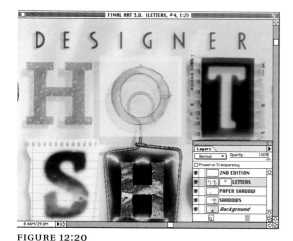

FIGURE 12:20

A Layer Mask can be used to vary the transparency of the objects on one layer.

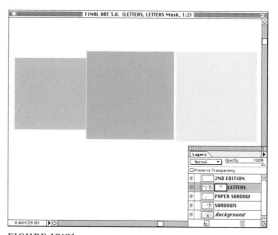

FIGURE 12:21

The Layer Mask previewed alone.

Output white point slider to the left—as you move the slider, the object selected in the layer will become more transparent. When you have the desired transparency, click OK (**FIGURE 12:19**).

4 Repeat steps 1–3 for any other objects you want to make transparent (**FIGURE 12:20**). You can also fill the selection with gray while the Layer mask is targeted—the level of gray determines the level of transparency. **FIGURE 12:21** shows the layer mask previewed alone.

If you decide to reposition the layer and you want to force the Layer Mask to follow the layer; double-click the Layer Mask preview icon and click the Layer radio button on under Position Relative To. Make sure there are no active selections—select the Move tool, target the layer, and click and drag.

If you want to move only one of the objects in the layer, you must move it and its mask separately. Draw a selection marquee around the object and click and drag it to a new position. Then, target the Layer Mask and turn its preview icon on in the Channels palette. With the Magic Wand, click on the object's mask to select it—the mask must be previewed or the magic wand will select pixels on the layer not the mask. Make sure the Background color is set to white, click and drag the mask, and position it with the object.

FADEOUTS   Layer Masks can have any level of gray, so they can be used to fade one image into another. If you apply a gradient fill to a layer's Layer Mask, the layer will be transparent relative to the mask's gradient fill. To fade one object into another:

1 Add a Layer Mask to the layer with the object to be faded. Use the Rectangular selection tool and make the selection surrounding the object.

2 Target the Layer Mask, and make a linear blend from black to white in the selected area. Where the blend is white, there is no effect on the layer. As the blend changes to black the layer becomes more transparent (**FIGURE 12:22**). Black hides the layer only if you have chosen the default setting of Color Indicates Hidden Area in the Layer Mask Options dialog box.

3 To alter where the break to transparency occurs, open Levels and adjust the middle Input slider. Moving the slider to the right reveals more of the object, moving it to the left hides more of the object (**FIGURE 12:23**).

 Depending on its complexity, a Layer mask adds some size to the file. Once you have made a final decision on the object's transparency and shape, you can remove a layer's mask and permanently apply the changes to the layer. Target the layer and choose Remove Layer Mask from the palette menu and you can choose whether to Apply or Discard the mask.

FIGURE 12:22

A Layer mask with a blend from white to black causes the object in the layer to fade out.

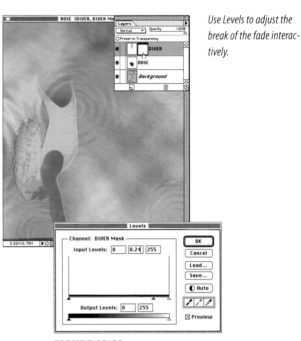

Use Levels to adjust the break of the fade interactively.

FIGURE 12:23

CLIPPING GROUPS

Another feature of the new Layers palette is clipping groups. A clipping group is made up of a base layer and one or more additional layers above the base. The transparent areas of the base layer mask the layers above—the base creates a window. I used a clipping group to create the illustration in **FIGURE 12:24**. The interior of the egg is made up of three layers grouped together. The base of the group is the interior of the egg filled with black on a transparent background that clips the objects in the two layers above (**FIGURE 12:25**). To make a clipping group:

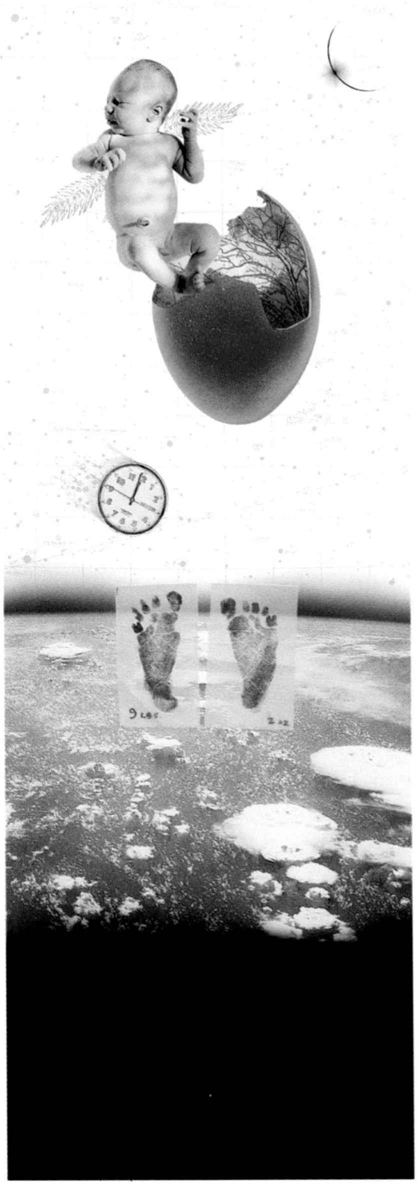

FIGURE 12:24

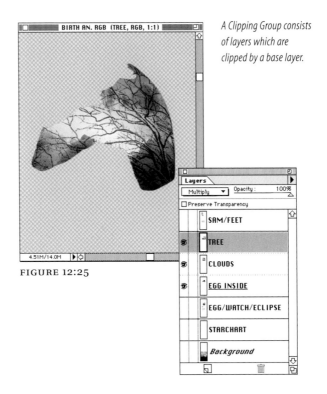

FIGURE 12:25

A Clipping Group consists of layers which are clipped by a base layer.

1 Any sequence of layers can be designated as a clipping group. I started the egg's clipping group by targeting the Egg layer and then clicking the New Layer icon to add a layer above the egg, which I named Egg Inside (**FIGURE 12:26**).

2 Using the Pen tool I made a path along the egg interior and converted it to a selection. With the Egg Inside layer targeted, I filled the selection with black (**FIGURE 12:27**). The fill can be any color; it is the transparent areas of the base layer that establish how the layers above will be clipped.

A new layer was added above the egg layer which I named EGG INSIDE.

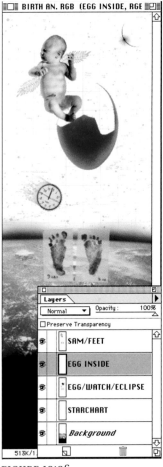

FIGURE 12:26

With the EGG INSIDE layer targeted, I selected the interior with the Pen tool and filled it with black.

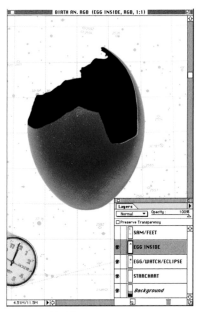

FIGURE 12:27

3 With the Egg Inside layer targeted, I clicked the New Layer icon again and this time checked the Group With Previous Layer box in the New Layer dialog box (**FIGURE 12:28**). I named this layer Clouds. When I clicked OK there was a dotted line between the Egg Inside and Cloud titles in the Layers palette, and the Egg Inside title was underlined (**FIGURE 12:29**). The dotted line indicates the layers are part of a clipping group.

4 I added another layer above the Clouds layer which I named Tree. In this case I also checked the Group With Previous Layer box. There was now a dotted line between each of the three new layers in the palette (**FIGURE 12:30**).

A New Layer was created and Group With Previous Layer was checked.

FIGURE 12:28

Another layer was added to the group named TREE.

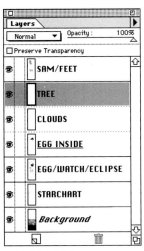

FIGURE 12:30

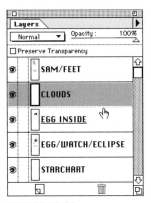

FIGURE 12:29

A dotted line between layers in the Layers palette indicates the layers are grouped.

5 Any objects that I pasted into the layers above the group's base layer would now only appear inside of the egg. I started by targeting the Cloud layer and copying and pasting a scan of clouds. The clouds appeared inside of the egg and were masked from the rest of the image (**FIGURE 12:31**). However, only the preview of the objects is masked and I could easily reposition or resize the clouds. If I clicked on the Cloud layer's Eye icon, I could view them unclipped (**FIGURE 12:32**).

6 I finished the clipping group by pasting a scan of trees against a white sky into the Tree layer. I changed the Tree layer mode to Multiply, which made the white sky transparent over the clouds (**FIGURE 12:33**).

The clouds in the CLOUDS layer were clipped by the EGG INSIDE layer.

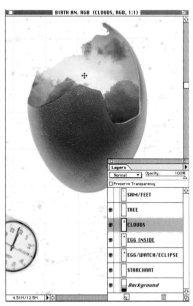

FIGURE 12:31

The CLOUDS layer viewed alone.

FIGURE 12:32

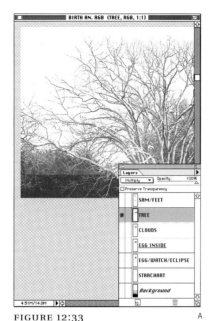

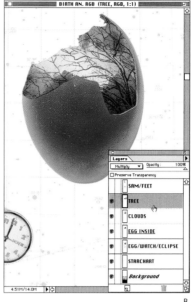

FIGURE 12:33 A   B

The trees were pasted into a layer, with its Mode set to Multiply (A). The Multiply mode made the white pixels transparent (B).

Option-clicking the line between two layers in the Layers palette adds the layer above to the group.

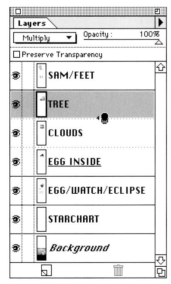

FIGURE 12:34

7 The clipping group gave added flexibility to the layer image as I could now edit the objects inside of the egg without being concerned about physically cropping them to the edge of the egg. I could also paste other objects or backgrounds into the layers of the group and move them around at will.

 You can also add layers into a clipping group by Option-clicking the line between the layer's titles in the Layers palette. Option-clicking again ungroups the layers (**FIGURE 12:34**).

IMPORTING FROM ILLUSTRATOR

13

As powerful as photoshop is at manipulating continuous-tone images, it can be very cumbersome if you want to create precise, flat color images with complex typographic elements. It is, however, quite easy to import Adobe Illustrator drawings into Photoshop. You can open an Illustrator file at any resolution as a grayscale, RGB, or CMYK color file. The imported Illustrator drawing is translated from object-oriented bezier curves into color or grayscale bitmaps at any desired resolution. Once an Illustrator file is bitmapped in Photoshop, you can manipulate it the same way you would any scanned image.

When you import Illustrator files into Photoshop, all the rules of scanned images apply—in most cases 1½ to 2 pixels per halftone dot is enough to render sharp edges. However, you should avoid importing finely detailed line art or typographic elements that are 100% of a color on a white background, if their edge appearance is important (see **FIG-URE 13:1**, *Imported Illustrator Resolution*). If you have grown tired of the flatness associated with object-oriented drawing programs, you can use Photoshop to add texture to the flat color. You can also combine the Illustrator drawings with photographs or artwork.

Imported Illustrator Resolution

Original Illustrator file   150 ppi   225 ppi   300 ppi

The rules for choosing resolution when importing from Illustrator are generally the same as for scanned continuous-tone images. The art should have between 1½ and 2 pixels per halftone dot. However, you should avoid type and line art on a light background. The figures above show the original Illustrator file and the file imported and separated out of Photoshop at resolutions of 150, 225, and 300 ppi, respectively. If the Illustrator art does include fine lines or type on a light background, a higher resolution should be used and Anti-aliased should be unchecked in the Rasterize Adobe Illustrator Format dialog box when the file is opened.

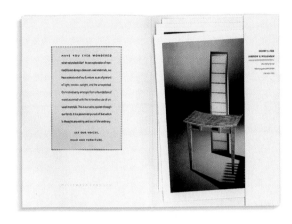

OPENING AN ILLUSTRATOR FILE

FIGURE 13:2 shows an illustration I started in Illustrator and finished in Photoshop. The illustration is for the cover of a folder for a custom furniture maker. In this case, I wanted to add some lighting effects to the hard-edged drawing which would be easier to accomplish in Photoshop.

Open an Illustrator file the same way as any other Photoshop file—choose Open from the File menu and choose an Illustrator file from the directory. When the Illustrator file is opened into Photoshop it is rasterized (converted into pixels). The Rasterize Adobe Illustrator Format dialog box (**FIGURE 13:3**) lets you specify the output size and resolution of the file when it is opened into Photoshop, the only limitation on size is your available RAM and disk space. You can also choose a color mode from the Mode pop-up menu. If you choose CMYK Color, then the

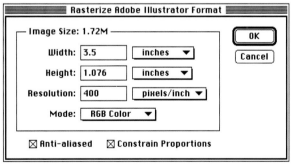

FIGURE 13:3

The Rasterize Adobe Illustrator Format dialog box lets you determine the resolution and color mode of the imported file.

Checking Illustrator Traps

Trapping creates a small amount of intermediate color between complimentary colors so that if the press goes off register a white space will not show between the colors. If you set your own traps in Illustrator it can be very difficult to double-check the traps because when you specify a color to overprint, Illustrator's preview is not affected. For example, if you overprint a 100% magenta shape on top of a 100% cyan shape, the printed result is dark blue (FIGURE A), while the previewed result is magenta (FIGURE B). If you open an Illustrator file in Photoshop as a CMYK file, any overprinted objects will preview as they will print (FIGURE C). If you have created traps in Illustrator by over-printing strokes or fills, open or place the file in Photoshop at a resolution high enough to show the width of the strokes (usually 200–300 ppi). You can then zoom in on the resulting Photoshop file and examine your traps (FIGURE D). If there is stroked type in the file you wish to check, you must first covert the type to outlines before opening it in Photoshop.

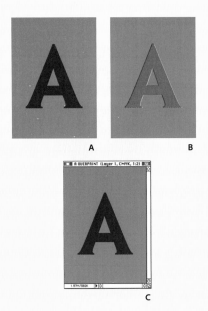

A B

C

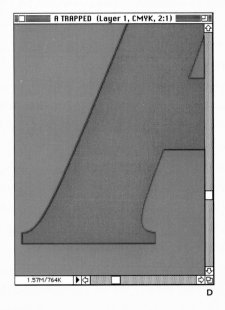

D

The Illustrator drawing opened as an RGB file.

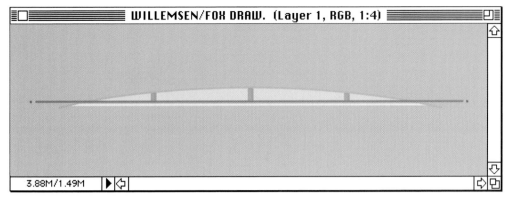

FIGURE 13:5

percentages you specified in Illustrator will be carried over to the Photoshop file (see **FIGURE 13:4**, *Checking Illustrator Traps*). Checking Anti-aliased smooths the edges of the drawing. Unchecking Constrain Proportions lets you adjust the horizontal or vertical scale of the drawing. Click OK, and the Illustrator drawing is rasterized and opened (**FIGURE 13:5**).

> **Photoshop's color management preferences affect the color of an Illustrator file when it is opened in Photoshop (see Chapter Fifteen, *Color Management*). For this reason the color you see in Photoshop may not visually match the colors you picked in Illustrator. You can adjust Illustrator's progressive colors to obtain better matches between the programs (see FIGURE 13:6, *Matching Illustrator and Photoshop Color*).**

Matching Illustrator and Photoshop Color

When you place or open an Illustrator file, its color in Photoshop will vary depending on what is entered in Monitor Setup and Printing Inks Setup in Photoshop's Preferences submenu under File. To improve the color matching between the two programs, you should start by matching Illustrator's progressive color patches to Photoshop's digitally. To match color between Illustrator and Photoshop:

1 Open Photoshop's General Preferences under File, and choose Apple from the Color Picker pop-up menu (FIGURE A).

2 Choose Printing Inks Setup from the Preferences submenu under file and choose Custom from the Ink Colors pop-up menu. Click on each color patch and record its RGB values from the Apple color picker (FIGURE B).

3 Open Illustrator and choose Color Matching from the Preferences submenu under file. Click on each color patch and enter the corresponding RGB values that you recorded from Photoshop (FIGURE C). If you are working with a calibrated monitor, this method will make your displayed Illustrator color more accurate; it will also change the displayed color of any existing drawings.

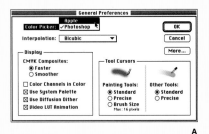

A

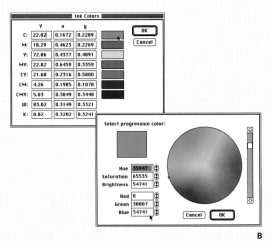

B

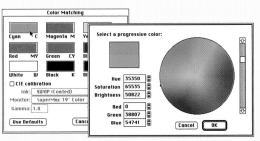

C

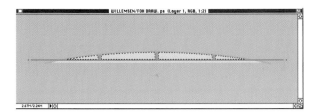

FIGURE 13:7

*With the Shift key pressed, I selected
each of the interior panels.*

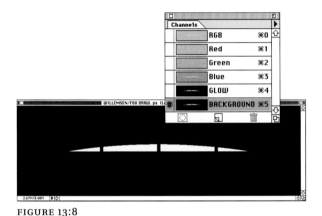

FIGURE 13:8

*Two new channels created from the
inverted Magic Wand selection.*

Once I had opened the Illustrator drawing I could
fine-tune its color and add the backlit effect by building a variety of masks. To add the glows:

1 I selected the four interior panels of the abstract
shape by setting the Magic Wand to a Tolerance
of 0 with Anti-aliased checked, and Shift-clicking
each panel (**FIGURE 13:7**).

2 Choosing Inverse from the Select menu, I
inverted the selection, and then saved the
resulting selection as two new channels by
clicking twice on the Convert to Selection icon
at the bottom of the Channels palette. I named
one of the channels Glow and the other Background (**FIGURE 13:8**).

3 I clicked on the Glow channel to view it, and
Option-clicked its title in the palette to load it
as a selection. With black as the foreground
color, I chose Stroke from the Edit menu, and
added a centered, 12 pixel stroke of solid black
(**FIGURE 13:9**).

4 I deselected (Command+D), chose Gaussian Blur
from the Blur submenu under Filter, set the
Radius to 10 pixels, and clicked OK (**FIGURE 13:10**).

FIGURE 13:9

The loaded GLOW channel with a 12 pixel black stroke added.

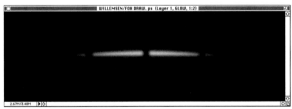

FIGURE 13:10

The GLOW channel with a 10 pixel Gaussian Blur applied.

5 In the Channels palette, I Option-clicked the Background title to load it as a selection, and filled the resulting selection with white (**FIGURE 13:11**).

6 Finally, I clicked on the RGB channel in the palette, Option-clicked the Glow title to load it as a selection, and filled the resulting selection with white (**FIGURE 13:12**).

To complete the backlit effect I added another glow to the top of the shape in a similar manner, converted it to CMYK, saved it as an EPS file, and placed it back into Illustrator where the type and rules were added (**FIGURE 13:13**).

 The correct stroke width or blur radius is dependent on resolution—a higher resolution file needs a wider stroke or radius to create the same effect.

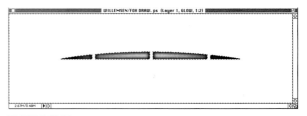

FIGURE 13:11

I loaded the BACKGROUND channel and filled the resulting selection with white.

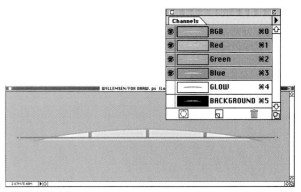

FIGURE 13:12

With the RGB composite targeted, I loaded the GLOW channel and filled it with white.

The Photoshop file imported back into Illustrator.

FIGURE 13:13

It is easier to set complex type in another program such as Illustrator and then import the type into Photoshop.

FIGURE 13:14

Duplicate lets you make a copy of the file with its layers flattened.

FIGURE 13:15

Change the duplicate file's mode to grayscale, and resample to 72 ppi.

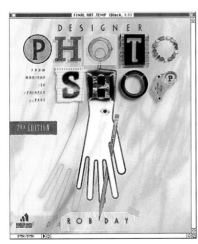

FIGURE 13:16

SETTING TYPE

Because Photoshop is a bitmap program, setting type of any complexity can be almost impossible. If you want to add type that consists of more than a few words to a Photoshop file, it is easier to first set the type in Illustrator, where there are no typographic constraints, and then place the type in Photoshop. I set some of the typographic elements for the cover of *Designer Photoshop* in this manner (**FIGURE 13:14**).

MAKING AN ILLUSTRATOR TEMPLATE   Before setting type in Illustrator, to be exported to Photoshop, it is helpful to make a template from the Photoshop file. You can use the template in Illustrator as a guide for setting type that will be exported to Photoshop. An Illustrator template previews as 1 bit per pixel, and its resolution is always 72 ppi. How a template is made in Photoshop makes a difference in the clarity of the template's preview when it is opened in Illustrator. To make an Illustrator template in Photoshop:

1 Choose Duplicate from the Image menu. The Duplicate Image dialog box lets you name the new file. I usually add the suffix .temp to the original file name (**FIGURE 13:15**).

2 Close the original file and convert the duplicate file to grayscale if it is in a color mode. Choose Image Size from the Edit menu and resample the image resolution to 72 ppi and then apply a strong Unsharp Mask (**FIGURE 13:16**).

3 Choose Bitmap from the Mode menu, Diffusion Dither as the Method, leave Output Resolution at 72 pixels/inch, and click OK (**FIGURE 13:17**).

4 Choose Save As from the File menu, PICT File from the Format pop-up menu, and click Save (**FIGURE 13:18**).

5 Launch Illustrator and choose Open from the File menu and open the Photoshop PICT file.

Choose Illustrator Template (PICT) from the resulting Open dialog box. **FIGURE 13:19A** shows the template as it appears in Illustrator with the drawing board at 100% magnification. **FIGURE 13:19B** shows the same original grayscale, saved as a PICT File, without first converting to a 72 ppi diffusion dithered bitmap.

6 I could now accurately set type in relationship to the jacket illustration (**FIGURE 13:20**).

Convert the grayscale file to a 72 ppi Diffusion Dither Bitmap.

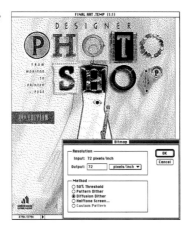

FIGURE 13:17

Save the 72 ppi bitmap image as a PICT File.

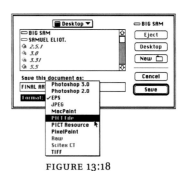

FIGURE 13:18

The 72 ppi Diffusion Dithered bitmap makes a template with more detail (A) than a grayscale file (B) when opened in Illustrator as a template.

FIGURE 13:19   A   B

You can also Place the original Photoshop file in Illustrator if it is saved in EPS format. The type can then be set while Preview is selected from the View menu. However, Illustrator's refresh rate will be slowed considerably in this case.

PLACING

Placing allows you to bring Illustrator objects directly into a Photoshop file—Illustrator's drawing board is treated as transparent when a file is placed. Place is not available in the File menu when the art is in Bitmap or Index Color mode. I set the type in Illustrator using the Photoshop template as a guide. The type was filled with black, the file was saved and placed back into the original Photoshop illustration as a

Quick Mask. I could then convert the resulting Quick Mask to a selection and fill it with any color or transparency. To place type set in Illustrator on a Photoshop image:

1 I opened the cover illustration and clicked on the Quick Mask icon so that the type would be placed in a channel and not on the actual file.

2 I chose Place from the File menu. An open dialog box appeared, allowing me to choose the Illustrator file.

3 An empty box with an x through it appeared and then a few seconds later a preview of the Illustrator art appeared inside of the box (**FIGURE 13:21**).

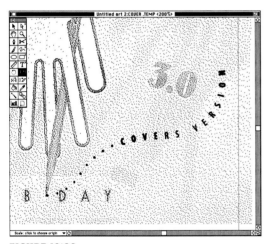

FIGURE 13:20

Using the template as a guide I set the type on a curved path and exported it to Photoshop.

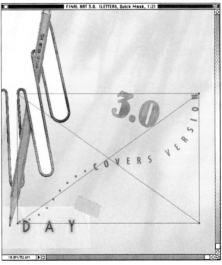

FIGURE 13:21

The Placed Illustrator type preview in a Quick Mask.

I could manipulate the preview's size, proportions, and position before placing a full-resolution version of the art.

4 Clicking and dragging on any of the corners of the preview will resize the art while constraining its proportions. If you want to distort the art, hold down the Command key while dragging the corner (**FIGURE 13:22**). To delete the preview, click once outside of the box.

5 When the cursor is on the x inside of the preview box it turns to a pointer; clicking and dragging on the x moves the art. When the cursor is anywhere else inside of the box it turns to a Gavel icon; clicking once with the Gavel places the finished high-resolution art (**FIGURE 13:23**).

Once the type was placed in the Quick Mask channel I could duplicate the mask, create a drop shadow mask, and then fill the masks with transparent color.

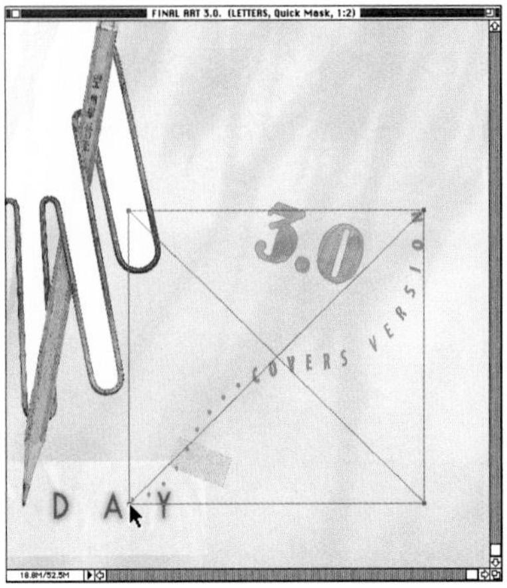

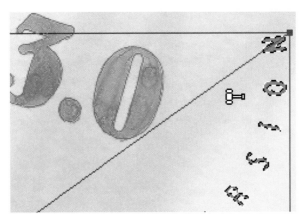

The preview can be resized before the final type is imported.

FIGURE 13:22

Clicking inside the preview box when the Gavel icon shows places the type.

FIGURE 13:23

Photoshop will not recognize patterned strokes or fills, or stroked type. An Illustrator pattern will open as a black fill. If you convert Illustrator type to outlines before opening it in Photoshop, then the strokes will be included. The Deluxe CD-ROM version of Photoshop ships with a shareware program called EPS Converter. This program lets you convert an Illustrator file with patterns and stroked type to a format that is readable in Photoshop. Also, Adobe Type Manager is used when type is rasterized and opened in Photoshop. If you are having problems with type not opening properly, try increasing ATM's font cache allotment in the ATM Control Panel.

IMPORTING AN ILLUSTRATOR PATH You can also import paths drawn in Illustrator and then save and edit them using the Pen tool. In Illustrator, open the Illustrator file you wish to import a path from, and copy the path to the clipboard (Command+C). Open a Photoshop file and paste (Command+V) the copied path and the Paste dialog box appears. You can choose Paste As Pixels, which functions in the same way as choosing Place does except you have no control over size and resolution, or you can choose Paste As Paths. In this case the copied path or paths are pasted into the Photoshop document as a new Working Path which you can name and save.

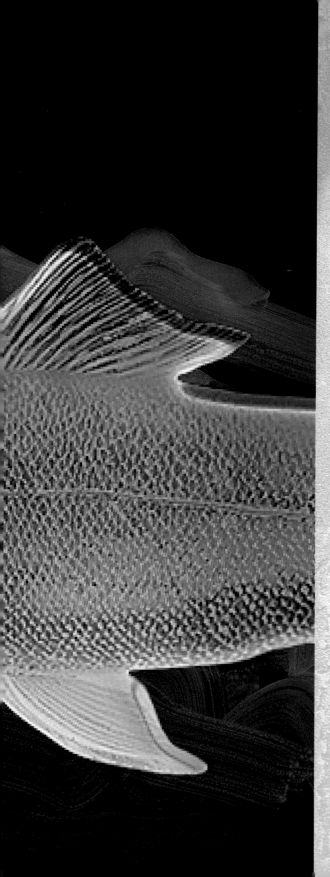

14
CALCULATIONS

Photoshop's calculate tools have a reputation as being off-limits to all but the most advanced users. Version 3.0 makes the calculate dialog boxes interactive with the image, making it easier for beginners to experiment and understand how these tools work. The dialogs are still very complex and can be off-putting when you first open them, but it is worth understanding how they work.

You can use the calculate tools for special effects—compositing images as if you were sandwiching positives and negatives on a light table—or you might use them as shortcuts for applying masks to an image or building new masks. In a production setting the calculate tools can be used with a macro utility such as Daystar's Photomatic to repeat often used channel operations. Most calculate functions can be duplicated by using layers with different Mode settings, or loading and manipulating various channels, but the calculate tools can be more efficient.

In version 3.0 the calculate tools are split into three items found under the Image menu named Duplicate Image, Apply Image, and Calculations. Choosing Duplicate Image simply duplicates the active window. You can choose to duplicate the document with or without its layers; this is very useful when you have a multi-layer document which you want to flatten and sample down before proofing to your printer.

Apply Image lets you perform calculations between two files that have the same pixel dimensions. One file is the Source, the other file is the Target—or the file to which the calculation will be applied. The target document is always the active window. Apply Image is a good starting point for learning about calculations since it usually involves only two documents (see **FIGURE 14:1**, *Apply Image Dialog Box*).

You use Calculations to build new mask channels by compositing two existing channels. With the Calculations dialog box you choose two channels from any same-sized documents, blend them together, and place the results as a new channel or selection in one of the documents. You can then use the resulting mask to further manipulate the image.

Apply Image Dialog Box

When you open the Apply Image dialog box (see accompanying figure), the targeted layer of the document you are working on (the active window) is the Target document, and any open document with the same pixel dimensions as the target file can be the Source. You can also choose to have another channel act as a mask by checking the Mask box. Here is an overview of the Apply Image dialog box:

- **SOURCE:** Any open document with the same pixel dimensions as the file you are working on can act as the source and will be blended with the target file. You can also specify a document's layers or channels to act as the source.
- **LAYER:** If the source is multi-layered, you can apply all the layers by choosing Merged or choose an individual layer.
- **CHANNEL:** You can choose to blend the composite color file or any of the file's individual channels. If you have chosen a layer from the Layer pop-up menu which has transparent areas, its transparent areas can be applied by choosing Transparency (FIGURE B).

- **INVERT:**   If you check the Invert box, the Source document's pixels are inverted when it is applied to the Target document. This is the equivalent of choosing Invert from the Map submenu under Adjust.
- **BLENDING:**   Click and drag on the Blending pop-up menu to choose a mode by which the Source document will be blended with the Target document (see FIGURE 9:38, *Color Modes*).
- **PRESERVE TRANSPARENCY:**   If the Target file is the layer of a document with transparent areas, you can protect the transparency of the layer from the effects of the blending by checking Preserve Transparency.
- **MASK:**   If you check the Mask box, then the dialog box expands to let you choose any channel from an open document to mask the effects of the blending. The black areas of the chosen channel mask the blending (FIGURE C).
- **RESULT:**   If there are no active selections in the Target file, holding down the option key when choosing Apply Image adds a Result pop-up menu. In this case you can send the blend of the two documents to a New Document, Layer, Channel, or Selection.

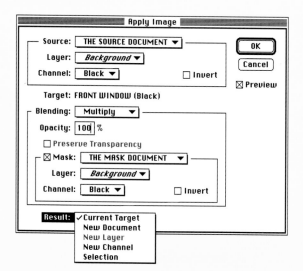

When you work with the calculate tools it is important to note that all of the documents you want to use must have the same pixel dimensions for them to show in the dialog boxes. A quick way to size two different documents so they have matching pixel dimensions is to make the largest document active, double-click the crop tool to open the Crop Tool Options palette, and check Front Image, which loads that document's dimensions and resolution in the palette. Now you can instantly size other documents to those dimensions by cropping them.

Two scans with the same pixel dimensions.

FIGURE 14:2

APPLY IMAGE

You can use Apply Image as a shortcut for a variety of tasks. For example, if you wanted to composite two images with the same dimensions together (**FIGURE 14:2**), the following method would work:

1 Click on the first document and choose All (Command+A) from the Select menu.

2 Copy the first document and click on the second document's window, then paste the copy of the first document.

3 Open the Layers palette, double-click Floating Selection, and the Layer Options dialog box appears. Choose an Opacity and a Mode by which the two layers will be blended , and click OK (**FIGURE 14:3**).

This method not only takes quite a few steps, but also requires using extra memory and time as you copy the entire image to the clipboard. You can perform the same composite in one step using Apply Image. Click on the image that you want to act as the target

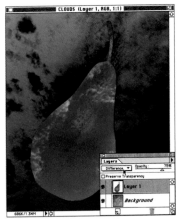

The two scans composited as layers with Difference as the Mode at 80% Opacity.

FIGURE 14:3

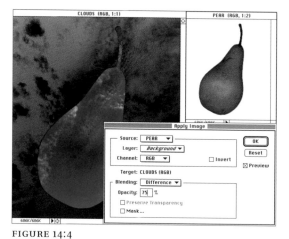

FIGURE 14:4

Two images can also be composited using the Apply Image dialog box.

FIGURE 14:5

Type set in a channel and then loaded as a selection can be ghosted using Levels.

(the bottom layer) and choose Apply Image. The second document will appear in the Source pop-up menu as long as it has the same pixel dimensions as the Target image. Choose RGB from the Channel pop-up menu, and a Blending mode and Opacity, and click OK. The first image is composited on the second (**FIGURE 14:4**). The disadvantage of this method is that the resulting image is permanently blended—it has only one layer and you would not be able to change your mind about the blending method later, but its file size will be smaller.

APPLYING CHANNELS   Apply Image can be even more useful when performing masking operations. For example, a common use of a channel mask is for ghosting type over a photograph. You can set the type in a new channel, load it as a selection, open Levels, and move the Output black point slider to the right to make the ghosted type (**FIGURE 14:5**).

You can also accomplish this task without actually loading the mask or opening Levels. Using Apply Image you can choose the RGB image as the Source, and the Type channel from the Channel pop-up menu. Check the Invert box and choose Screen from the Blending pop-up menu. An Opacity setting of 50% is the equivalent of moving the Levels Output white point slider half way to the left using the former method (**FIGURE 14:6**). A

75% Opacity is the same as moving the slider three-quarters of the way to the left, and so on. Or, if you wanted to darken the type you could choose Multiply with Invert unchecked. This is the equivalent of moving the Levels white point Output slider to the left with the selection loaded (FIGURE 14:7).

APPLY IMAGE AND MASKS   When you use Apply Image to composite two documents, you can blend the Source document through a mask. Check the Mask box at the bottom of the Apply Image dialog and the dialog will expand to include pop-up menus, allowing you to choose a channel that will act as the mask (FIGURE 14:8). This feature can make applying channels to an image even more efficient. I could have used Apply Image through a mask to create the glow on the Willemsen & Fox folder in fewer steps than described on page 181. To make the glow with Apply Image:

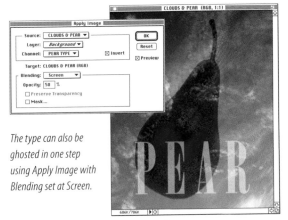

The type can also be ghosted in one step using Apply Image with Blending set at Screen.

FIGURE 14:6

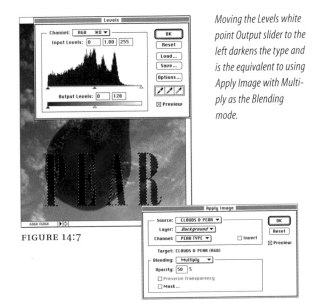

Moving the Levels white point Output slider to the left darkens the type and is the equivalent to using Apply Image with Multiply as the Blending mode.

FIGURE 14:7

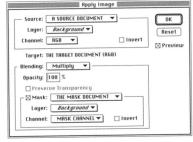

Checking the Mask box in the Apply Image dialog box lets you designate a channel which masks the blending.

FIGURE 14:8

1 I created the two mask channels for the imported Illustrator drawing as before (**FIGURE 14:9**).

2 Choosing Apply Image I made the drawing the Source, chose the Glow mask from the Channel pop-up menu, and checked the Invert box. Then I chose Screen from the Blending pop-up, left Opacity at 100%, and made the Mask Channel the Background mask (**FIGURE 14:10**).

3 I clicked OK. The Background channel masked the Glow channel as the Screen was applied to the image (**FIGURE 14:11**).

By using Apply Image I was able to skip steps 5 and 6 of the described masking technique. I could also easily modulate the intensity of the glow by changing the Screen Opacity.

APPLY IMAGE RESULT If there are no selections loaded in the Target file, you can hold down the option key while choosing Apply and a Result pop-up menu will be added to the Apply dialog box. Using Result you can change the target to a New Document, Layer, Channel, or Selection. For example, if you had a selection loaded in one document and wanted to duplicate that selection into another document, you

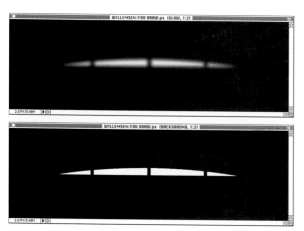

FIGURE 14:9

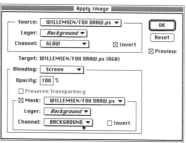

FIGURE 14:10

The Source is the GLOW channel inverted. The Blending mode is Screen and the BACKGROUND channel is designated as the Mask.

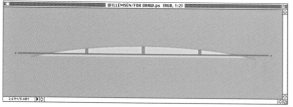

FIGURE 14:11

The GLOW channel applied to the image.

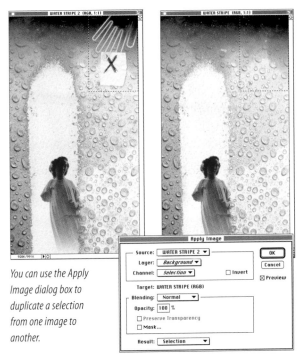

You can use the Apply Image dialog box to duplicate a selection from one image to another.

FIGURE 14:12

could setup the Apply Image dialog as shown in **FIG-URE 14:12**. The image with the selection to be duplicated is the Source, the Channel is Selection, Blending is Normal 100%, and the Result is Selection. Click OK and the selection from the first document is loaded into the second document.

CALCULATIONS

The Calculations dialog box (see **FIGURE 14:13**, *Calculations Dialog Box*) functions differently than Apply Image in two ways. The blending is always performed between two single channels—you can't composite color images together using Calculations. Also, you choose an existing or new channel as a des-

Calculations Dialog Box

The Calculations dialog box (FIGURE A) lets you blend two individual channels together to create a new channel or replace an existing channel. You can use Calculations to build complex channel masks which can be loaded as a selection into a document or applied to a document via Apply Image. Here is an overview of the Calculations dialog box:

- **SOURCE 1 AND 2:** The channels of any open documents with the same pixel dimensions can act as the two source channels that will be blended together.
- **LAYER:** If the source is multi-layered, you can apply all the layers by choosing Merged or choose an individual layer. If you choose a layer, its transparent areas are treated as black.
- **CHANNEL:** You can choose to blend any of the document's channels. If the document is color, each of its color channels will be available; you can also choose Gray which is the equivalent of converting the color image to grayscale. If an individual layer is chosen from the Layer pop-up menu, you can choose Transparency as the channel. In this case the completely transparent areas are blended as black and the completely opaque areas are blended as white. If there is an active selection in the document, you can choose Selection as the channel.
- **INVERT:** If you check the Invert box, the

Source document's pixels are inverted when it is blended with the other Source. This is the equivalent of choosing Invert from the Map submenu under Adjust.

• **BLENDING:** Click and drag on the Blending pop-up menu to choose a mode by which the two Source Channels will be blended together (see FIGURE 9:38, *Color Modes*).

• **MASK:** If you check the Mask box, then the dialog box expands to let you choose any channel from an open document to apply as a mask to Source 1. In this case it is as if you had loaded the Mask Channel as a selection in Source 1's Channel and filled the selection with black.

• **RESULT:** Choose a document from the Result pop-up menu as a destination for the blend of the two Source Channels. If you choose New from the Channel pop-up menu, the result will be added as a new channel to the document. You can also choose an existing channel; in this case the blended result will replace the chosen channel. Choose Selection if you want the result loaded as a Selection.

• **PREVIEW:** Check the Preview box to see a preview of the Result. If you choose Selection from the Result Channel pop-up menu, the preview shows as a grayscale representation of the resulting selection where white is open and black is closed.

A

tination for the resulting composite of the two source channels—the front window is not necessarily the target as it is with Apply Image. You can use Calculations to perform a variety of tasks from loading multiple channels to building complex masks.

SIMPLE CALCULATIONS   When you load a channel as a selection, Photoshop 3.0 lets you add, subtract, or intersect the channel with an active selection via the Load Selection dialog box. When you use the Load Selection dialog in this manner you are performing simple calculations. For example, if want to load two channels together as one selection, you can first load one of the channels, and then choose Load Selection again, choose the second channel to be added from the Channel pop-up menu, and click on Add to Selection (see FIGURE 10:11). You could also load the two channels as a selection in one move by choosing Calculate and setting up the dialog box as shown in **FIGURE 14:14** with Add as the Blending mode. Likewise, you can intersect or subtract the

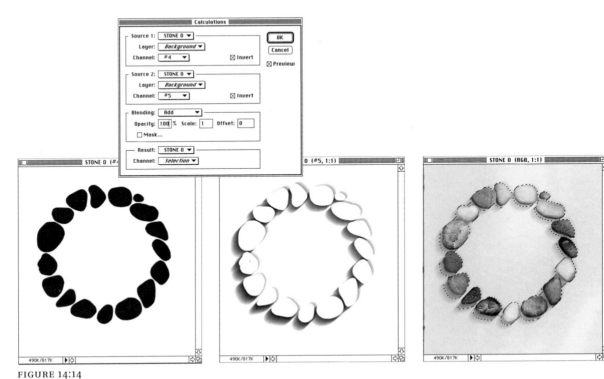

FIGURE 14:14

The Calculate dialog box can be used to load two channels at once.

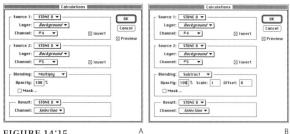

FIGURE 14:15   A   B

Two channels can be intersected and loaded as a selection (A), or one can be subtracted from the other and loaded as a selection (B) using Calculations.

two channels using the Calculate dialog with the Blending mode set at Multiply and Subtract, respectively (**FIGURE 14:15**). Using the Calculate dialog you have the option of loading the channels as a selection, or saving the combined channels to a new channel.

Another simple calculation is to choose two of the RGB channels as the Sources, check the Invert boxes for both Sources, and choose Multiply as the Blending mode. This makes a mask of the image's shadow areas; you can then apply the Unsharp Mask filter to bring more details out of the shadow areas without affecting the highlights (**FIGURE 14:16**).

FIGURE 14:16

The Calculate dialog box can be used to quickly select an image's shadow areas by multiplying two of the RGB channels and setting the Result Channel pop-up to Selection. Here I have applied the Unsharp Mask filter to the shadow areas to reveal more detail.

BUILDING COMPLEX MASKS   The Calculate dialog can also be used to create complex masks for creating three-dimensional effects—from simple drop shadows to imitation chrome. For example, to create a drop shadow:

1 Select the object that you want to make the shadow for and save the selection (FIGURE 14:17).

2 Duplicate the saved channel and apply a Motion Blur (FIGURE 14:18).

3 Choose Offset from the Other submenu under Filter, enter a Vertical and Horizontal offset amount, and click OK (FIGURE 14:19).

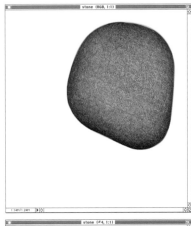

Start the drop shadow mask by selecting the object and saving the resulting selection.

FIGURE 14:17

Duplicate the saved selection and apply a blur filter. In this case I have used Motion Blur which gives the appearance of two different light sources when the shadow is applied.

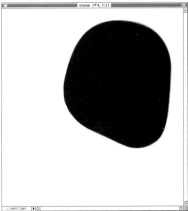

FIGURE 14:18

Apply the Offset filter to the blurred channel.

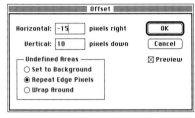

FIGURE 14:19

4 Choose Calculate and make Source 1 the saved selection, Source 2 the blurred copy inverted, Blending mode Multiply, the Result as Selection, and click OK. You can now use Levels to darken the selected shadow area (**FIGURE 14:20**).

Calculation masks can be much more complex than simple drop shadows and the possibilities are endless. By blurring and offsetting saved selections you can create highlight and shadow mask and affect surfaces such as chrome and metal. On the next page **FIGURES 14:21** and **14:22** show some recipes for more complex calculated masks.

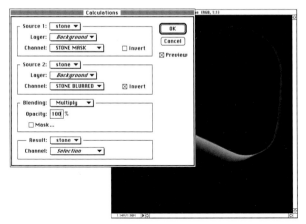

FIGURE 14:20

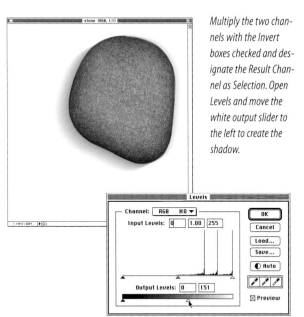

Multiply the two channels with the Invert boxes checked and designate the Result Channel as Selection. Open Levels and move the white output slider to the left to create the shadow.

Drop shadows can be made to look more realistic if they appear to have more than one light source. The stone in figure A was scanned directly on a flatbed scanner, selected, and then the Lighting Effects filter found in the Render submenu under Filter was applied to make the stone appear to be lit from above (B). The selection was saved to three new channels (C). Two of the channels were blurred, one with Gaussian Blur and the other with Motion Blur (D). I named the two channels SHADOW 1 and SHADOW 2 and gave them different preview colors.

Previewing the RGB and blurred channels together, I targeted the two SHADOW channels and repositioned them using the Move tool (E). I then calculated the two channels with Soft Light as the Blending mode at 70% Opacity and the Result as a New Channel (F). With the resulting channel targeted, I applied the STONE MASK inverted with Screen as the Blending mode (G). Finally, I loaded the channel as a selection, opened Levels, and adjusted the white Output slider of the individual RGB channels to color the two-way shadow (H).

A

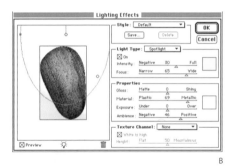

B

C

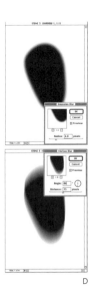

D

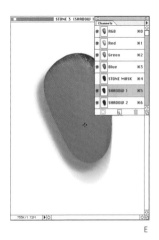

E

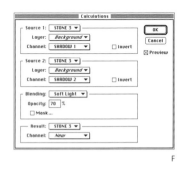

F

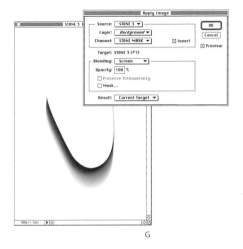

G

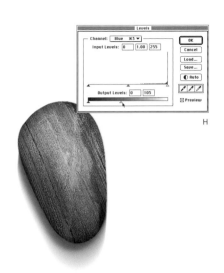

H

A   B   C   D

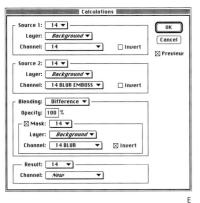

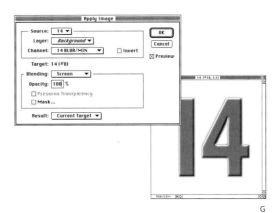

E   F   G

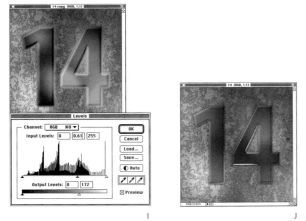

H

I   J

You can use the Calculations dialog box to create an endless array of surfaces. Here I have created a raised metallic effect by calculating the four channels in figures A – D. I started by setting the number 14 in a channel and duplicating the channel. I then applied the Gaussian Blur filter to the duplicate channel (B), and duplicated it twice. The Emboss filter was applied to one of the duplicate blur channels (C), and Minimum filter was applied to the other (D). The filter amounts that you apply are dependent on resolution, so you will have to experiment.

Figure E shows the Calculations dialog for calculating the difference between the unaltered 14 and the embossed 14, with the blurred 14 used as a mask, resulting in a new channel (F). I inverted the new channel and applied the 14 BLUR/MIN channel (D) using Screen as the Blending mode to delete the gray background (G).

Finally, I loaded the 14 BLUR/MIN channel (D), and with the RGB channel targeted I filled the selection with a light yellow, deselected, and applied the Lighting Effects filter to the entire image (H). I loaded the calculated channel (G) as a selection and used levels to adjust the shadows and create the 3-D effect (I). You can also experiment calculating various shadow and highlight masks, loading them as selections, and applying Lighting Effects (J).

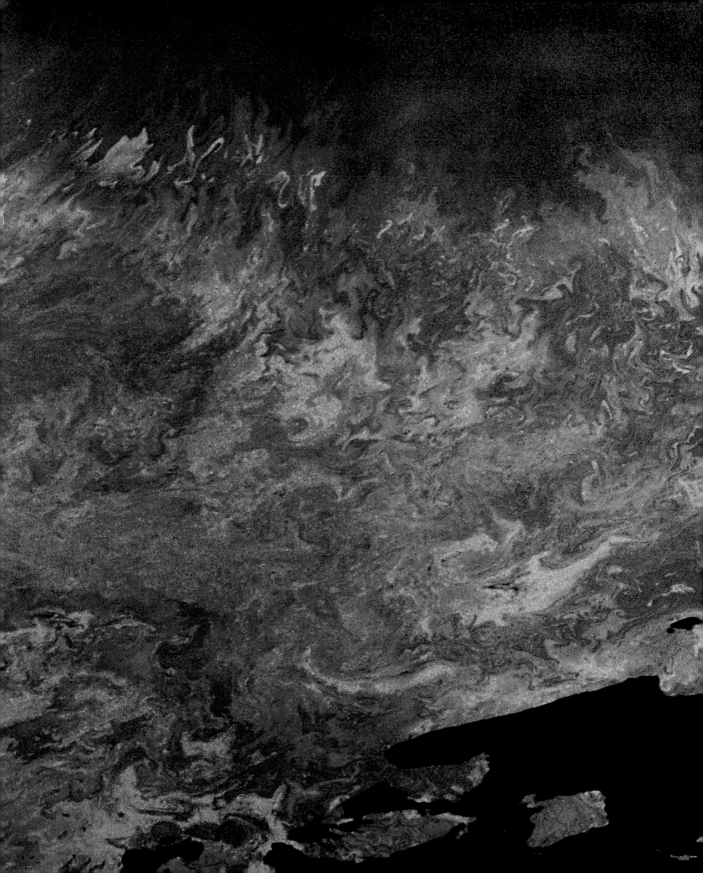

COLOR MANAGEMENT

IF YOU MAKE COLOR CORRECTIONS to a Photoshop file based on what you see on you monitor, then you must manage the way color is output if you have any hope of the printed color matching the displayed color. All monitors display the same RGB values differently depending on the monitor's characteristics—gamma, white point temperature, phosphors, and ambient light (see Chapter Two, *Working Conditions*). Likewise, all printers output the same CMYK values differently depending on their characteristics—dot gain, gray balance, and ink colors. The interaction of various display and output device characteristics can be infinite.

When an image is converted from RGB to CMYK mode, Photoshop accounts for the display and output device's character via the Monitor and Printing Inks Setup preferences. Making RGB to CMYK conversions can be a dilemma for a designer who does not want to be responsible for making a separation—but it is the best way of getting accurate color relative to the your display. If you send an RGB file to your service bureau and let them make the separation, chances are the color will not be what you intended, since your monitor and the service bureau's will have different characteristics.

How closely the output matches your display depends both on your working conditions and how carefully you adjust the Monitor and Printing Inks Setups found under the Preferences submenu. Your monitor and any output devices are limited in how much of the visible color spectrum can be displayed or printed—this is often referred to as the color gamut. It is important to understand the color limitations of both displays and output devices, so that you don't choose colors that cannot be printed.

COLOR GAMUTS

Before starting to build profiles for your monitor and different output devices, you should have a basic understanding of RGB and CMYK color. Monitors and process ink on paper deliver color to our eyes differently. Because of deficiencies in the purity of monitor phosphors and printing pigments, both the displayed RGB and printed CMYK color have limited gamuts relative to the visible spectrum. Fortunately almost the entire CMYK gamut lies within the RGB gamut, making it possible to an get accurate preview of the printed piece on your monitor (**FIGURE 15:1**).

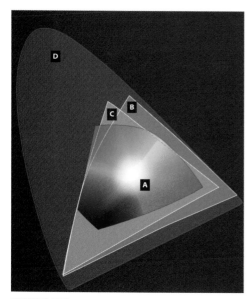

FIGURE 15:1

All input, output, and display devices have a color gamut, or range of possible color, that is a subset of the entire visible spectrum. CMYK color (A) has a very narrow range of color relative to all visible color (D). Photographic film (B) and RGB monitors (C) have a larger gamut of color, but their gamuts are still much narrower than visible color. Because the entire gamuts of visible color, monitor color, and film color cannot be printed, the unprintable parts of their gamuts are represented here as gray.

RGB COLOR The color displayed on your monitor is called additive color (see **FIGURE 15:2**, *RGB and CMYK Color*). Red, green, and blue are the primary additive colors—by adding varying combinations and intensities of these three colors, a large gamut of colors can be produced. The RGB monitor's gamut is very large, but it cannot come close to displaying the entire visible spectrum. Also, there are some CMYK colors that cannot be displayed accurately on an RGB monitor (for example, 100% cyan), even though the CMYK gamut is much narrower than the RGB gamut.

Since the RGB gamut is larger than the CMYK gamut, there are many displayed colors that cannot be printed by four-color process. If you expect to match output to your display, you cannot use the out-of-gamut colors in the RGB model. Photoshop provides a number of tools for dealing with RGB colors that are out of gamut:

- **GAMUT WARNING:** New to Photoshop 3.0, Gamut Warning indicates out-of-gamut colors with a color overlay—choosing Gamut Warning from the Mode menu activates the overlay choosing it again deactivates the overlay (see **FIGURE 8:14**).

- **CMYK PREVIEW:** Also new to version 3.0, CMYK Preview lets you preview the CMYK color without actually converting from RGB to CMYK. Selecting CMYK Preview from the Mode menu adjusts the preview of an RGB file to show how it will print based on the Monitor, Printing Inks, and Separation Setups. Choosing CMYK Preview again returns the image back to the full RGB preview.

- **COLOR RANGE:** Color Range lets you select the out-of-gamut colors in an image and then color correct them. Choose Color Range from the Select menu, set the Fuzziness to 0, and choose

RGB and CMYK Color

Light is made up of varying wavelengths, which we perceive as color depending on the wavelength's frequency. Red has the longest visible wavelength and violet the shortest. White light can be divided into three primary colors—red, green, and blue. A monitor's display is divided into small cells containing red, green, and blue phosphors that, when stimulated with electricity, emit combinations of red, green, and blue light. When your monitor adds the RGB colors together at full intensity, the result is white on your display (FIGURE A). If only two of the RGB colors are combined at full intensity, a new color is created. FIGURE B shows how adding only the red and green parts of the spectrum at full intensity results in yellow. By adding different combinations and intensities of the RGB colors, your monitor is capable of displaying a wide range of color.

CMYK ink on paper works in a very different way from your monitor's RGB phosphors. Depending on the pigment's color, the ink absorbs or reflects parts of the visible spectrum. Yellow ink absorbs (subtracts) the blue part of the spectrum and then reflects red and green light back to our eyes, which we perceive as yellow (FIGURE C).

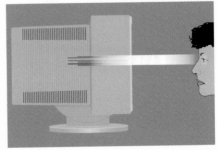

A

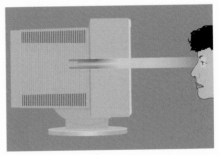

B

C

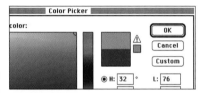

FIGURE 15:3

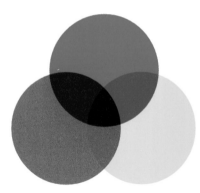

FIGURE 15:4

Out of Gamut from the Select pop-up menu to select any out-of-gamut colors.

• **COLOR PICKER EXCLAMATION POINT:** When you select color with Photoshop's Color Picker, occasionally an exclamation point with a small color patch beneath it appears next to the newly selected color in the Color Picker's dialog box. The exclamation point indicates that the selected color is not printable with CMYK ink; the small patch indicates the closest printable color (**FIGURE 15:3**). Clicking on the exclamation point replaces the current out-of-gamut color with the closest printable color. The exclamation point also appears in the Info palette.

CMYK COLOR   The color model of the printing press is CMYK color. CMYK is called subtractive color (**FIGURE 15:2C**). Ink on a printed page absorbs or reflects different wavelengths (colors) of light depending on the pigment. The wavelengths that are reflected back to your eye are perceived as different colors. When the three subtractive primaries (CMY) are combined at 100%, the result is close to black (**FIGURE 15:4**). This is because most of the visible colors in the spectrum are being subtracted by the pigment, while very little is reflected. Because of the impurities in the pigments of CMY printing inks, a perfect black cannot be made when cyan, magenta, and yellow are combined; therefore black must be added as a fourth color.

 CMYK printing is generally referred to as subtractive color, but strictly speaking it is a complex mix of both additive and subtractive color. For example, when 50% magenta and 50% yellow halftone dots are mixed, they appear orange. The two pigments absorb some light and reflect the rest. Because the dots are small we do not perceive them individually as magenta and yellow, but as an additive combination of the two—orange.

Photoshop allows you to edit images in either CMYK or RGB mode. When you work in CMYK mode, you are given an RGB color preview to work with, and as you work, the four CMYK channels are edited. The accuracy of the CMYK file's RGB preview is dependent on correct Monitor and Printing Inks Setups.

There are some situations that warrant working in CMYK mode. High-end scanners make excellent conversions from RGB to CMYK (see FIGURE 8:13, *Comparing Scanners*). When you buy a CMYK scan from a service bureau or trade shop, you should work in CMYK mode to retain the benefits of the scanner's conversion. However, if you are changing color radically, chances are you will lose the high-end scanner's conversion benefits. In this case, RGB is faster (the file size is smaller) and, as described below, working in RGB mode and then making the conversion to CMYK with Photoshop gives you more control matching color from different output devices.

LAB COLOR   Lab is a Photoshop color mode which is device independent. Lab is a theoretical mapping of all visible color—it has no gamut limit since it is not displayed or printed (FIGURE 15:5). Think of Lab color as the Rosetta Stone of color—Photoshop uses Lab as a reference point when making the translation from displayed color values (RGB) to printed color values (CMYK). How accurately the conversion is made for a given device depends on the settings entered in the Monitor and Printing Inks Setups found in the Preferences submenu under File (see FIGURE 15:6, *How Photoshop Uses Lab Color*). The Monitor Setup settings are a profile of your display, and the Printing Inks Setup settings are a profile of the device you intend to output the file from. If both preferences are set correctly, then the preview of a CMYK file will predict the printed color. Understanding how these preferences work is essential for getting accurate color from a variety of devices.

*The Lab color model defines a color along three axes. **L** is luminance, a color's lightness or darkness; **a** is the color's hue from red to green across the color wheel; and **b** is the color's hue from yellow to blue across the color wheel.*

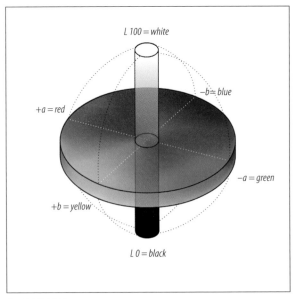

FIGURE 15:5

How Photoshop Uses Lab Color

Both RGB and CMYK color are dependent on the devices that they are displayed on, or printed from. The same RGB values appear visually different depending on the characteristics of the display, and also the same CMYK values print as different colors depending on the characteristics of the output device.

To allow you to account for the various device characteristics, Photoshop uses the Lab Color mode when converting an image from RGB to CMYK, or from CMYK to RGB. Lab color is device independent—it is a mapping of all visible color and is neither printed nor displayed, so it has no gamut limitations. When you convert an RGB file to CMYK, the RGB values (FIGURE A) are first converted to corresponding Lab values. The Lab values are adjusted depending on the settings in Monitor Setup, which ideally make an accurate profile of your specific monitor (FIGURE B). The adjusted Lab values (FIGURE C) are then converted to CMYK values. The CMYK values are adjusted depending on the settings in Printing Inks Setup, which should be a profile of the specific output device that the file will be sent to (FIGURE D). If the Monitor and Printing Inks Setups are accurate profiles of the display and specific output device, then the resulting output will match your display within the limitations of the device's respective gamuts (FIGURE E). You can then save one master RGB file, separate it using different Printing Inks Setups depending on the output device, and get back similar color from each device you use.

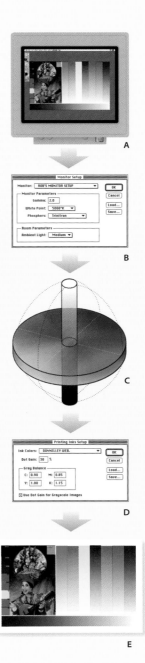

MONITOR SETUP

The Monitor Setup preference can be potentially confusing in that you are not actually adjusting your monitor, you are merely telling Photoshop *how* you have adjusted the monitor—you are creating a monitor profile. The Monitor Setup dialog box lets you choose Monitor, Gamma, White Point, Phosphors, and Ambient Light settings (**FIGURE 15:7**). The settings you choose should be a reflection of the kind of monitor you use, the gamma and white point you have chosen for your display using a hardware calibrator or the Gamma Control Panel Device provided with the Macintosh version of Photoshop, and the ambient light of your work space (see Chapter Two, *Working Conditions*). This information is used to adjust a CMYK file's preview without adjusting the actual CMYK values that are sent to the printer. Or, if the file is in RGB Mode, the preview is not adjusted, but the CMYK values that the RGB file will be converted to are adjusted. To correctly adjust your Monitor Setup preferences:

1 Choose Monitor Setup from the Preferences submenu under File. Click on the Monitor pop-up menu and choose your monitor's make from the list. If your monitor is not available choose Other.

2 Enter your monitor's gamma in the Gamma box. If you use a hardware calibrator, enter the gamma you set the monitor to using the calibrator's software. If you do not use a hardware calibrator, use the Gamma CDEV provided with Photoshop and set your monitor's gamma to between 1.8 and 2.2, then enter that number in Monitor Setup's Gamma box.

3 Enter your monitor's white point temperature in the White Point box. If you use a hardware calibrator, enter the white point you set the monitor to using the calibrator's software (between 5000°K and 6500°K). If you do not use a hardware calibrator and have used the Gamma CDEV to adjust the monitor's white point to visually match white paper, choose 5000°K as the White Point. Also, many monitors now ship with a cor-

The Monitor Setup is a profile of your monitor's characteristics.

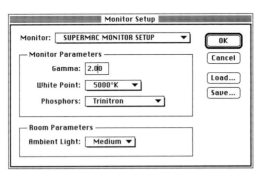

FIGURE 15:7

rected white point to remove the blue cast (see FIGURE 2:3), in which case enter your monitor's specified white point.

4 If you were able to choose your monitor from the Monitor pop-up menu, then its phosphor set will automatically be chosen in the Phosphors pop-up menu. If you chose Other, then choose your monitor's phosphor set from the Phosphor's pop-up menu. Almost all monitor makes use one of the sets listed—Trinitron is the most common.

5 Choose either Low, Medium, or High from the Ambient light pop-up menu to match your room's lighting conditions.

PRINTING INKS SETUP

Once you have established the profile for your monitor in Monitor Setup, it is important to also build profiles for any output devices you use. The Printing Inks and Monitor Setups work in unison to give you a correct RGB to CMYK conversion for almost any monitor and output device combination. They also give you an accurate on screen representation of how an image will print from a specific device once it is in CMYK Mode (assuming that both the display and output device are consistent over time).

Photoshop provides generic profiles for the most commonly used output devices, which are found in the Printing Inks Setup's Ink Colors pop-up menu (**FIGURE 15:8**). These profiles assume that your Monitor Setup is in fact an accurate profile of your monitor and working conditions, and that the specified output device will perform as expected. However, with so many variables at work (your monitor's phosphors may change due to age, its gamma might actually be 1.7 when you think it is 1.8, the printer's dot gain might actually be 23% when it is assumed to be 20%, and so on) the provided printer profiles may not produce accurate results. For this reason it is important to adjust the Printing Inks Setup based on a visual comparison of a target print, output from the devices that you use; to an on-screen display of the CMYK file used to make the target print. For best results the target should be viewed under 5000°K light

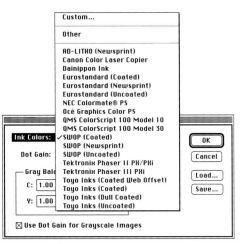

Printing Inks Setup's Ink Colors pop-up menu provides generic profiles for the most common printers.

FIGURE 15:8

as different light sources can alter the target's color (**FIGURE 15:9**).

FIGURE 15:9

Color changes appearance depending on the temperature of the ambient light. Fluorescent light can make a color seem bluer, while incandescent light can make the same color appear yellower.

OLÉ NO MOIRÉ   Adobe provides a CMYK file for making target prints found in the Calibration folder named Olé No Moiré (**FIGURE 15:10**). This file has a full range of color and gray values, and it has 100% patches of the CMY colors and their overprint combinations. I have found that it is also useful to add gradient blends for each of the CMY colors and their overprints, from 100% to 0% (**FIGURE 15:11**). To make the blends: select a rectangular area, set the foreground color to 100% of the color, the background color to white, and use the Gradient tool with its options set at the defaults. Make a blend from top to bottom.

 It is very important that the file used to make a target print is not altered in any way before output. It is essential that the CMYK file you compare on screen, to the target, is the same file that was used to make the target print.

You can make a custom profile for any printer using Printing Inks Setup, from inexpensive inkjet printers, to web presses. If you are making film separations and providing your client with a laminate proof made from the film, such as a 3M Match Print, or Chromalin, then the target print should be output from the imagesetter and proofing combination you will use in final production. It is also worthwhile making custom profiles for any printers that you use to make make pre-film proofs, such as Canon copiers, or Iris printers. You can then have one master RGB file that is separated differently depending on the output device, and as a result, get matching output from a variety of devices.

FIGURE 15:10

The Olé No Moiré file can be used as a target for making a custom printer profile.

FIGURE 15:11

Adding ramps of the primary colors to Olé No Moiré can be a useful reference when making a printer profile.

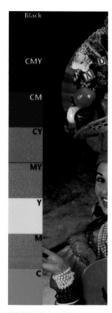

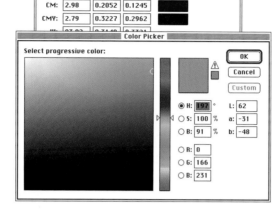

FIGURE 15:12

The Ink Colors dialog box lets you adjust the CMY color patches and their overprint colors to match the target print's corresponding patches.

Some dye-sublimation printers print without using a black plate (they only use CMY) and will only take RGB files. Film recorders also work in this manner. You cannot build printer profiles for these devices.

BUILDING A PRINTER PROFILE

Once you have had target prints output from the devices you will be using, you can start to build custom Printing Inks Setups for each device. The targets should be illuminated under 5000°K light and then Printing Inks Setup's Ink Colors, Dot Gain, and Gray Balance settings should be adjusted until the on-screen preview of the target file matches, as closely as possible, the printed target.

INK COLORS   Start by clicking on the Ink Colors pop-up menu and choosing Custom from the top of the list, which opens the Ink Colors dialog box. This dialog shows ink patches for the CMYK inks and their overprints—CMY, CM, CY, and MY. Olé No Moiré has corresponding patches running down its left side (**FIGURE 15:12**). Clicking on any of the patches opens a color picker which lets you alter the preview of the patch as necessary. It is important to note that cyan is out of gamut to an RGB display, so you will not be able to get a precise match for the cyan patch. You should be able to get very good matches for the overprint colors, and in this case having blends on the target will be very helpful in judging the colors—particularly the CMY patch, which is very important in the display of neutral colors. When you have adjusted the patches, click OK to return to the Printing Inks Setup dialog; click OK again and the preview of the target print will be adjusted.

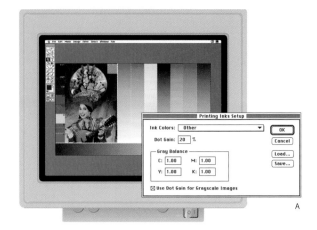

 Adjusting the ink patches is very important for eccentric printing conditions, such as a web press on newsprint, where the hue and saturation of the inks can vary widely (some printers use a magenta that is closer to red). In these cases it is wise to have a target that is proofed from the press.

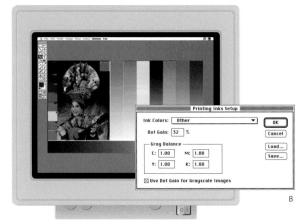

DOT GAIN When an image is printed its halftone dots usually gain in size when the plates are inked, making the image appear darker. The Dot Gain setting lets you darken or lighten the CMYK file's preview to simulate the printed image on screen. Open Printing Inks Setup again and compare the on screen preview to the proof. The patches on the left side of the print should be a closer match, but the preview may still appear too light or dark. If the preview is too light, increasing the Dot Gain setting will darken the preview when you click OK. Adjust the Dot Gain percentage until the overall lightness or darkness of the preview matches the print (**FIGURE 15:13**).

FIGURE 15:13

Adjusting the Dot Gain setting darkens or lightens the preview of a CMYK file. The web press that printed this book has more dot gain than a sheet fed press. Increasing the Dot Gain setting darkens the CMYK preview (B) to match the printed target (C).

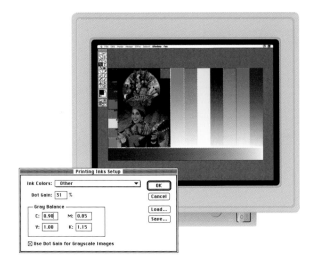

FIGURE 15:14

By adjusting the Gray Balance setting you can add more or less of the CMYK colors to the preview.

Because Printing Inks Setup and Monitor Setup interact with each other, the Dot Gain setting you arrive at via visual comparisons may not be the value your printer claims to get on press. Setting the Dot Gain by visual comparison to a target lets you account for inaccuracies in the monitor's profile or your printers expectation of dot gain on press.

GRAY BALANCE   The final step in creating a printer profile is to adjust the Gray Balance. Gray Balance lets you adjust for the dot gain of the four colors separately. There are four boxes labeled C, M, Y, and K with default settings of 1.00. Lowering a number adds more of that color to the on-screen preview. If the target print appears to have too much red compared to the preview, then lowering the M number will add more magenta to the preview and make it appear redder (**FIGURE 15:14**). Olé No Moiré's gray background is a good guide for setting the Gray Balance. Once you have adjusted the Gray Balance you may have to fine-tune the Dot Gain setting.

Unfortunately the adjustments you make in Printing Inks Setup are not interactive, so you have to open and close the dialog box to see the results. You can find the correct Gray Balance settings interactively by using Levels. Make sure to set the Gray Balance numbers in Printing Inks Setup to the default 1.00 and click OK. Open Levels and adjust the color by using only the middle Input slider for each of the channels separately. Be careful not to make an adjustment to the composite CMYK—you must select the channels individually by choosing them one at a time from the Channels pop-up menu (**FIGURE 15:15**). When you have matched the preview to the target print, note the number in the middle Input Levels box for each channel and click *cancel* (it is important that you do not apply this Levels adjustment to the target file). Reopen Printing Inks Setup and enter the noted Levels numbers in the corresponding Gray Balance boxes and click OK.

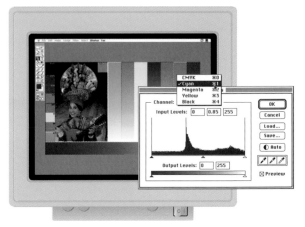

FIGURE 15:15

You can use the middle slider of Levels to determine the Gray Balance numbers interactively. Be sure not to apply the Levels setting to the image—record the numbers, cancel, and enter the numbers in Printing Inks Setup's Gray Balance dialog.

Once you have matched the CMYK preview to the target print, any CMYK file you open will preview as it would print from the device profiled in the Printing Inks Setup. If necessary you can now accurately color correct those files based on what you see on the screen (**FIGURE 15:16**). Also, if you convert an RGB file to CMYK, the CMYK values are accurate for the device

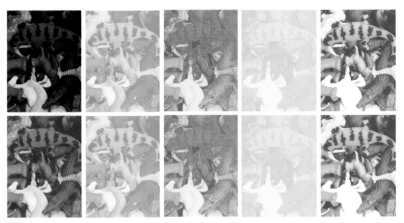

FIGURE 15:16

When you load different Printing Ink, Monitor, or Separation Setup preference settings while an image is in CMYK mode, its preview will change, while its underlying CMYK values remain the same.

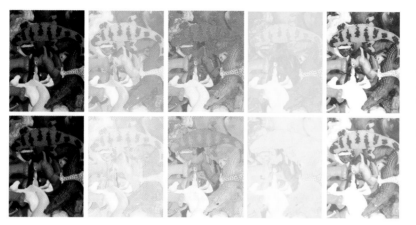

FIGURE 15:17

When you convert an image from RGB to CMYK using different Printing Ink, Monitor, or Separation Setup preference settings, its preview remains the same, but its underlying CMYK values change.

profiled in the Printing Inks Setup (**FIGURE 15:17**). When you convert to CMYK the preview will not change unless there are out-of-gamut colors, or the black plate has been severely limited via the Separation Setup preference (see *Ink Limits*, page 220). You can save one master RGB file, and convert it to CMYK using each devices' profile and get back similar color.

SEPARATION SETUP

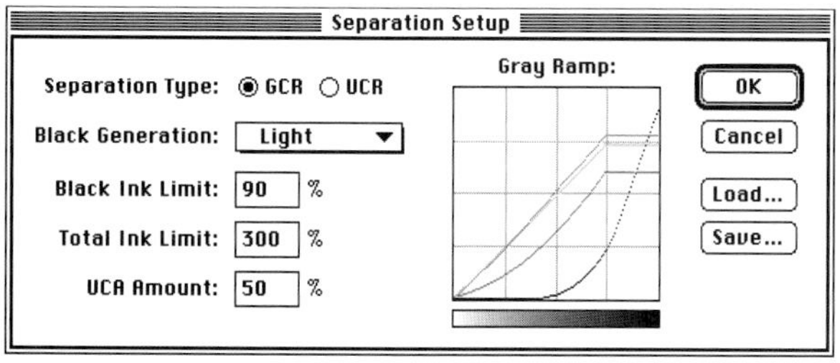

FIGURE 15:18

The Separation Setup dialog box lets you determine how the black separation is made.

When you make a CMYK separation, there is a third set of preferences that affect the way the conversion is made. Converting from RGB to CMY is a relatively simple process, but generating the black plate is more problematic since it must be interpolated. The information that you enter in the Separation Setup dialog box determines how the black separation is made (**FIGURE 15:18**). How the black separation is made can affect how the image will perform on press, so different press conditions require different black generations. If you are not familiar with these issues, then check with your printer on how to set the Separation Setup.

GCR AND UCR Gray Component Replacement (GCR) and Under Color Removal (UCR) are two separation strategies that replace some of the CMY color with black. This makes the color on press more predictable and manageable, and it can also save ink costs (black is the least expensive of the four inks, which can be significant in long runs). GCR is Photoshop's default; it employs a method by which the color that adds definition and shape to the image is replaced with black. For instance, if a fleshtone is made primarily with magenta and yellow and its shadows are defined with cyan, some of the cyan is replaced with black. This theoretically makes the fleshtone less susceptible to unwanted color shifts on press.

UCR removes gray colors made with all three CMY colors and replaces them with an appropriate percentage of black ink. UCR is often used for difficult press conditions such as printing on newsprint. GCR is the method many separators prefer because it allows more control in making the black plate. Ask your printer which method he or she prefers.

BLACK GENERATION Black Generation dictates how much density there is in the black plate when you make a GCR separation. There are five options available: None (makes a CMY-only separation), Light, Medium, Heavy, and Maximum. Medium is the default but many printers prefer a lighter black plate. You can also choose Custom from the Black Generation pop-up menu and modify the Black Generation curve. Different Black Generation settings will have little effect on color, but will affect press performance.

INK LIMITS You can limit the overall density of the ink coverage and the maximum density of the black ink by adjusting the Total Ink Limit and Black Ink Limit percentages. The default setting for Total Ink Limit is 300%; this means that the maximum combined percentages of the four inks will never exceed 300% in any given part of the image. When the total ink density exceeds 300% on a four-color press, the ink might not dry properly and there is the risk that the ink will offset onto another sheet. Some presses can handle more or less ink coverage, so check with your printer.

The Black Ink Limit allows you to adjust the maximum percentage of black ink that is generated. The default setting is 100%. Most printers prefer a Black Ink Limit of between 85% and 95% so that the shadows don't fill in on press.

UCA AMOUNT Under Color Addition (UCA) allows you to add color back in that has been removed via the GCR process. The default setting is 0%. If your separations are printing flat in the shadow areas, adding some color back in (20% to 50% is usually adequate) can add some richness to the shadow areas.

 Adjusting the Separation Setup has no effect on the preview of an existing RGB or CMYK file. It does affect the CMYK values that an RGB file will be converted to, and when the conversion is made, the preview might be altered depending on the settings. For example, if the Black Ink Limit is severely limited, then the shadows of the preview might be lightened.

SAVING A SEPARATION TABLE

You most likely will want to output your files from a number of different devices, so it is important to save the profiles you make in Printing Inks Setup. You should make a folder for storing saved Printing Inks Setups. Clicking the Save button in Printing Inks Setup lets you name and save a profile; clicking Load lets you load the saved profiles.

If you want to save a Printing Inks Setup and a Separation Setup together, you can make and save a Separation Table. Load the Printing Inks and Separation Setup preferences you want to save as a table and choose Separation Tables from the Preferences submenu. Click save, name the table, and save it to disk. You can then load the saved table before making a conversion for the device profiled in the table. Loading a saved table overrides the current preference settings with the ones saved in the table.

POST-CONVERSION CORRECTIONS

When you convert from RGB to CMYK, the CMYK preview might look different from the original RGB file if you have used out-of-gamut colors. There can also be slight tonal shifts in the shadow areas if the black plate has been severely limited in Separation Setup. Once the conversion is made, you may want to fine-tune the final CMYK image; here are some things to look out for in the final CMYK file:

- If the color has shifted due to out-of-gamut colors, you may want to attempt to color correct those areas of the image. Once you are in CMYK Mode, you will not be able to choose out-of-gamut colors.

- Check the highlight areas. Only images with highly reflective objects (such as chrome or glass) should have pure white areas. The highlight areas that are bright white usually should have a mix of CMY at between 3% and 5%. Neutral highlights usually have more cyan in the mix. Use Select Color to correct highlight areas (see FIGURE 6:24).

- Check highly saturated colors; for example, bright red should be made of high percentages of magenta and yellow, and black or cyan should only be used to define shadow areas and details.

- Because 100% cyan is out-of-gamut to an RGB monitor the on-screen preview of highly saturated blues can be inaccurate. Make sure that the CM patch in Printing Inks Setup is visually accurate.

GRAYSCALE PROFILES

You can choose to allow the Dot Gain setting in Printing Inks Setup to affect the preview of a grayscale image by checking Use Dot Gain for Grayscale Images. As is the case with CMYK files, only the preview is altered—the print values remain the same. This allows you to adjust the preview of a grayscale to match a target print. If you do not check Use Dot Gain for Grayscale Images, then the preview you see for grayscale assumes your monitor is calibrated and the press conditions are normal (normal dot gain on coated paper). Leaving Use Dot Gain for Grayscale Images unchecked will not be as accurate as checking

A target print for determining the Dot Gain setting for grayscale images.

FIGURE 15:19

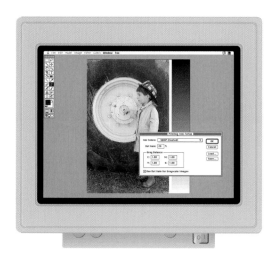

FIGURE 15:20

Compare the preview of the file to the printed output.

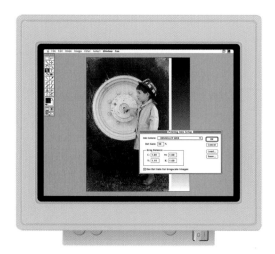

FIGURE 15:21

Adjust the Dot Gain setting until the preview matches the output.

it and setting the Dot Gain percentage based on a target comparison. To make an output device profile for grayscale:

1 Make a test file of a grayscale image that includes a full range of grays. You might want to include a grayscale bar, which you can make by selecting a rectangle and filling it with a blend from white to black (**FIGURE 15:19**).

2 If you can afford it, output the test file as a film negative from the imagesetter that you will be using, and have your printer run a press proof from the negative. If you cannot afford a press proof, have a black-only color proof made. This will predict some dot gain that might occur on press. You could also have a contact print made of the negative, but this will not predict any dot gain.

3 Preview the test file on your monitor. Choose Printing Inks Setup from the Preferences submenu, check Use Dot Gain for Grayscale Images, and click OK. Compare the test file to the test print. Adjust the preview by increasing or decreasing the Dot Gain percentage in Printing Inks Setup (**FIGURE 15:20**).

4 When you have matched the preview (**FIGURE 15:21**), save the new Printing Inks Setup by clicking Save. Name the file and save it in your Printing Inks Prefs folder.

5 Load the saved Printing Inks Setup preferences for the printer you will be using before you edit your grayscale scans.

 If Use Dot Gain for Grayscale Images is checked in the Printing Inks Setup dialog box, it affects the preview of grayscale images without affecting the data. Do not edit grayscale images without first loading the proper Printing Inks Setup.

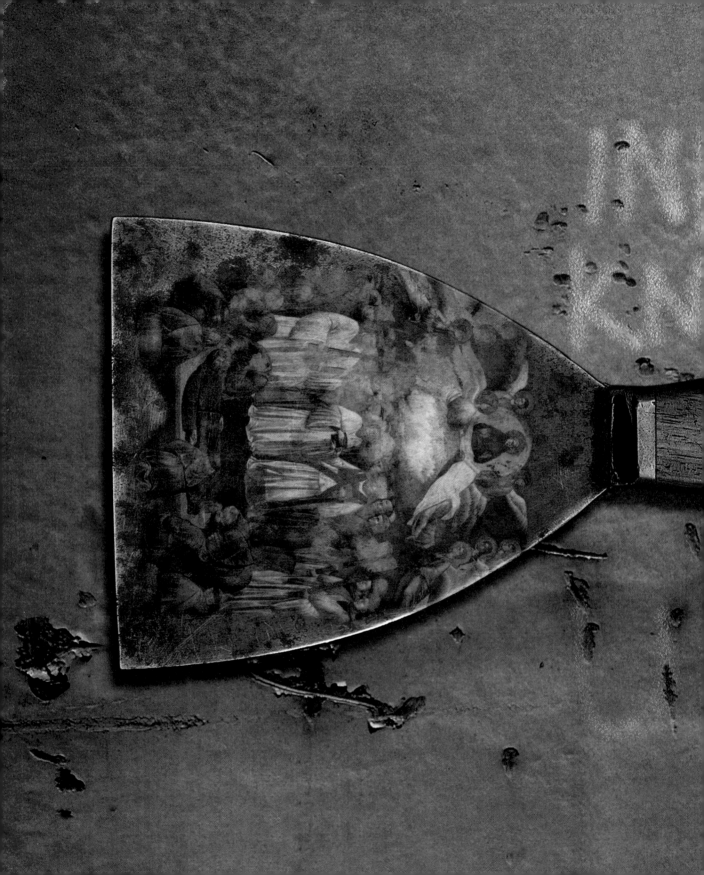

MIXING CUSTOM INKS

16

Once you understand the underlying concepts behind Photoshop's Printing Inks Setup, it is possible to specify
and mix custom (non-CMYK) colors.
Photoshop has a Duotone Mode which
lets you convert a grayscale image into a
duotone, tritone, or quadratone (see
FIGURE 16:1, *Duotones*). The duotone
mode is limited in that it uses the same
grayscale image with different curves
applied for each color when it is output.
For example, it would be impossible to
select an area of a duotone and fill the
selection with only one of the colors.

Photoshop's Duotone Mode allows you to apply different curves (see FIGURES 6:8–6:13) to one grayscale image and then separate the file accordingly. The resulting plates are then printed with different colored inks. You can apply curves and assign ink colors to as many as four plates. Open a grayscale image, choose Duotone from the Mode menu and choose Monotone, Duotone, Tritone, or Quadratone from the Type pop-up menu in the Duotone dialog box. You can then click on the Ink color patches to get a color picker and assign a color to the plate. Click on the Ink's corresponding curve icon to adjust the color's curve (FIGURE A). Because a Duotone mode document has only one channel, you cannot select an area and fill it with specific percentages of the colors.

Traditionally, duotones are used to extend the possible tonal range of black and white images on press. This is accomplished by printing with two plates, one with black ink and the other with gray ink. Different tonal curves are applied to the image to create the

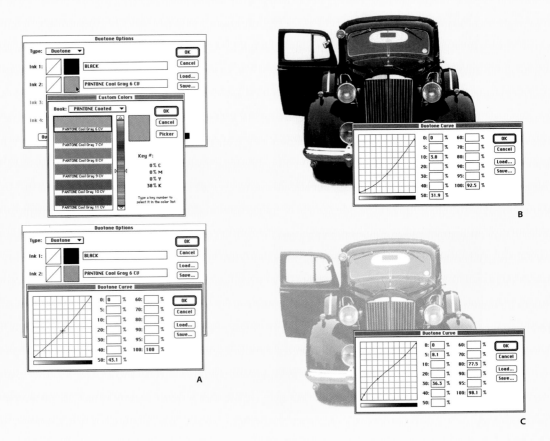

Black only

Quadratone   D

plates. For example, a curve that would increase contrast and suppress the highlight areas might be applied to the black plate (FIGURE B), while a straighter curve might be applied to the gray plate (FIGURE C). In this case the high-contrast black plate adds definition to the image, particularly in the shadow areas; while the gray plate increases the tonal range of the image. The tonality of an image can be extended even further by creating tritones or quadratones, applying different curves to each plate, and printing them with different values of gray ink. FIGURE D compares the image printed with black only to a quadratone using CMYK inks.

You can also use duotones to add a color tint to an image by printing the second plate with a color that has more saturation. In this case the black plate might be straighter, while the steepness of the second color's curve would determine how much color was added to the image (FIGURE E).

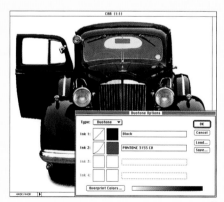

E

It is possible to edit an image in CMYK Mode and accurately view how that image would print using ink colors other than CMYK. Because CMYK Mode is multi-channeled (Duotone mode uses only one channel), there is no limit to how an image can be edited using the chosen colors. You should have a solid understanding of Photoshop's color management tools covered in Chapter Fifteen, particularly Printing Inks Setup, before attempting to use this method for a real world project.

CHOOSING CUSTOM INKS

As I mentioned in Chapter Fifteen, part of the process of building a good printer profile is adjusting the Ink Colors in Printing Inks Setup to visually match, as closely as possible, corresponding printed patches as viewed under 5000°K light (see FIGURE 15:12). The patches found in Printing Inks Setup's Ink Colors dialog box are not limited to any hue, saturation, or value—you can pick any color within the gamut of your RGB monitor. Any changes you make to these patches will be reflected in an image's CMYK preview.

If the monitor preview is to be accurate to the printed sheet, the colors you choose to replace any of the C, M, or Y patches in Ink Colors must visually match a printed swatch of color. You must also specify accurate overprint colors. Overprint colors indicate how any combination of the primary colors will mix. In the Ink Colors dialog box they are labeled MY, CY, CM, and CMY. Adjusting the overprint colors is critical if the preview is to be accurate.

 If your job has only two colors, one of which is black, then no overprint color needs to be specified, since 100% black combined with any color prints as black. Printing two-color jobs, where black is one of the colors, is a safe way to start experimenting with custom ink colors.

USING DUOTONE MODE TO CHOOSE OVERPRINT COLORS

FIGURE 16:2 shows a three-color book jacket I illustrated for *The Marriage Diaries of Robert and Clara Schumann,* published by Northeastern University Press, using two Pantone colors and black. For this project I replaced the cyan patch with green (Pantone 3288), the magenta patch with orange (Pantone 164), and the cyan/magenta patch with the two Pantone color's overprint values as specified in Duotone Mode. To specify accurate custom colors and their overprint colors, it is necessary to start in Duotone mode. The Duotone Options dialog box enables you to find accurate overprint colors, which can then be digitally specified in the Printing Inks Setup. To choose custom colors and their overprint combinations:

1 I opened a new document in Grayscale Mode and chose Duotone from the Mode menu. I selected Duotone from the Type pop-up menu.

The Marriage Diaries of Robert and Clara Schumann, *printed with two Pantone colors and black. Design by Virginia Evans, art direction by Ann Twombly, Northeastern University Press.*

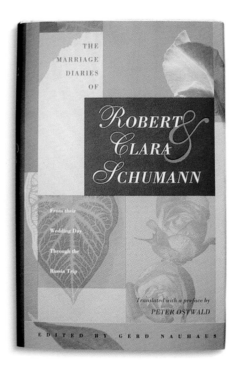

FIGURE 16:2

2 Clicking on the Ink 1 color patch opens the Photoshop color picker. You can click on Custom to choose a specific color from a number of custom color libraries. Clicking on the Book pop-up menu lets you choose a library. In this case I chose Pantone Coated and typed 3288 to find the green ink color, then clicked Picker to return to the Photoshop color picker (**FIGURE 16:3**). The color picker shows the Lab values for the chosen color, which I noted (48L, -61a, 2b, in the case of Pantone 3288) and clicked OK.

3 I then clicked on the Ink 2 color patch and repeated step 2 specifying Pantone 164 as the second color (**FIGURE 16:4**).

4 Finally I clicked on Overprint, clicked on the 1+2 patch, and noted the overprint color's Lab values (32L, -23a, 32b in this case) and clicked OK (**FIGURE 16:5**).

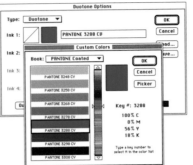

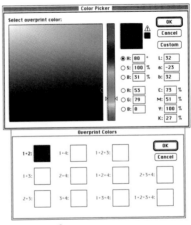

Click on the Ink 1 color patch to open the color picker. If you chose a custom color, click Picker to return to the Photoshop color picker and note the color's Lab values.

FIGURE 16:3

Get the Lab values for the second ink color.

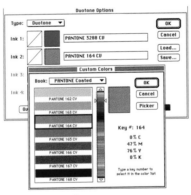

FIGURE 16:4

Note the Lab values for the overprint color.

FIGURE 16:5

Choose Custom from Printing Inks Setup's Ink Colors pop-up menu.

FIGURE 16:6

ADJUSTING THE PRINTING INKS SETUP
Once I had determined the Lab values for the two custom colors and their overprint color, I could easily transfer the colors to the Printing Inks Setup. With the Printing Inks Setup's color patches adjusted, I could then edit an image in CMYK Mode and view it as it would print using the chosen colors. To transfer the Lab values:

1 Choose Printing Inks Setup from the Preferences submenu and choose Custom from the top of the Ink Colors pop-up menu (**FIGURE 16:6**).

2 Click on the cyan patch and enter the Lab values that you noted for the first ink color in Duotone Mode in the corresponding L, a, and b boxes (**FIGURE 16:7**). The color you replace cyan with should have the darkest value of the chosen custom colors.

3 Click on the magenta patch and enter the Lab values for the second color (**FIGURE 16:8**).

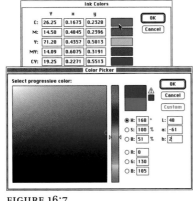

Click on the C patch and enter the Lab values you noted for Ink 1 in the Color Picker dialog box.

FIGURE 16:7

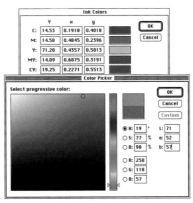

Click on the M patch and enter the Lab values you noted for Ink 2 in the Color Picker dialog box.

FIGURE 16:8

4 Click on the CM patch and enter the Lab values you recorded for the overprint color and click OK (**FIGURE 16:9**).

 Make sure you save your new Printing Inks Setup so that you can easily revert back to a normal CMYK setting and then back to the custom ink set. Click the Save button, name the setup, and save it to a desired folder. Choosing SWOP Coated from Ink Colors resets the Printing Inks Setup to its defaults (**FIGURE 16:10**).

FINE-TUNING THE CUSTOM COLORS
Depending on how accurate you need the printed color to be, you may decide to fine tune the custom ink patches. If you have setup your work space and calibrated your monitor as described in Chapter Three, you can compare your on-screen custom ink patches to corresponding printed swatches viewed under 5000°K light. You may find that it is necessary to adjust the patches in Printing Inks Setup to visually match the swatches.

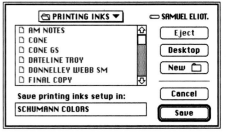

Click on the CM patch and enter the Lab values you noted for the overprint color of Ink 1+2 in the Color Picker dialog box.

FIGURE 16:9

Save the custom Printing Inks Setup so that you can easily reset the dialog box to a normal CMYK ink setting and then load the custom ink setting later if necessary.

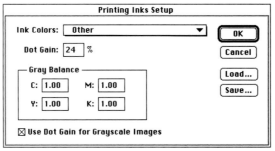

FIGURE 16:10

There are some Pantone colors that are out of gamut to your RGB display. If you chose an out-of-gamut custom color, you will not be able to match the displayed patch to the printed swatch. In this case the file's preview may not be accurate.

Pantone also publishes a *Color Tint Selector* which can be very helpful in fine-tuning a custom color. The book shows each Pantone color tinted at 10% increments. I make a CMYK file with corresponding tint blocks in each of the four channels and compare the on-screen preview to the printed Pantone tints (**FIGURE 16:11**). If necessary I adjust the color patches and the Dot Gain setting until I get a good match.

USING A TARGET PRINT   If the project has a high enough budget, it can be worthwhile having a target proof made using your custom colors. Chromalin makes a color proofing system that allows any custom color to be specified. I output Olé No Moiré as a film separation and then have a custom Chromalin made from the film where the C, M, or Y films are proofed using the corresponding colors that I have specified in Printing Inks Setup (**FIGURE 16:12**). I use this target as a reference for fine-tuning the Printing Inks Setup (see Chapter Fifteen, *Color Management*).

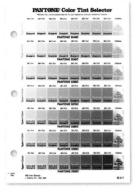

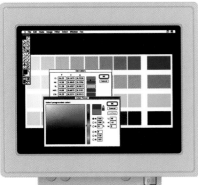

FIGURE 16:11

Pantone's Color Tint Selector can be a useful reference for visually adjusting the custom ink patches.

FIGURE 16:12

Olé No Moiré proofed with the two Pantone colors and black.

EDITING A CUSTOM INK FILE

Once you set up a custom Printing Inks Setup, any editing you do on the custom color job must be done in CMYK Mode. You must also make sure that any of the CMYK channels that are not being used remain blank—in the case of the Schumann jacket I did not use the yellow channel. If you attempt to cut and paste RGB images into a custom color CMYK file, its color will be altered and all four channels will be used. I created the Schumann illustration by pasting grayscale images into only the CMK channels (**FIGURE 16:13**). I could then open Levels and adjust the channels individually to alter the color (**FIGURE 16:14**).

 Photoshop's Picker and Swatches palettes are altered to reflect the Printing Inks Setup's Ink Colors. You will still be able to pick any RGB color for the foreground and background colors, but if you use them in the image they will be clipped to fall within the gamut of the custom colors you have chosen in Printing Inks Setup.

EXPORTING A CUSTOM INK FILE If you wish to export a custom color file and add other colored elements, Adobe Illustrator also lets you adjust its progressive ink patches. Use the method described in FIGURE 13:6, *Matching Illustrator and Photoshop Color,* to match the ink patches between the programs. Once you have adjusted the ink colors in Illustrator to match the custom ink colors you specified in Photoshop, you can save the Photoshop file in EPS format (see Appendix A, *File Formats*) and place it in Illustrator. Any objects you color with CMYK percentages in Illustrator will also preview as they will print when replaced with the chosen Pantone colors. Again

I pasted grayscale scans into the cyan, magenta, and black channels and then adjusted the color with the color correction tools.

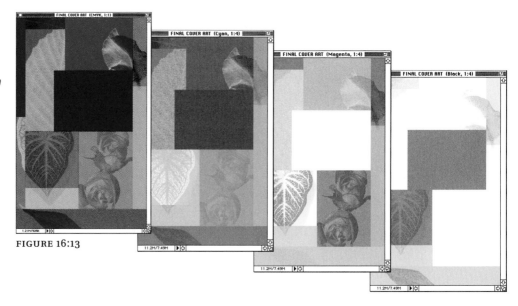

FIGURE 16:13

you should take care to use only the CMYK channels you used in Photoshop—in this case I could not use yellow in my color mixes (**FIGURE 16:15**).

 The color patches in Illustrator are saved in the Adobe Illustrator Prefs file located in your System Folder's Preferences folder. If you want to save the custom color patches you specify in Illustrator, quit Illustrator after adjusting the patches and copy the Adobe Illustrator Prefs file into another folder along with the job. If you want to reload the patches later, copy the saved Adobe Illustrator Prefs file back into the System's Preference folder.

OUTPUT AND PROOFING

The finished file should be output as a CMYK separation, but only the channels you use need to be output—for the Schumann jacket I output only the cyan, magenta, and black films. If your service bureau or printer can make a custom color laminate proof, proof the films replacing the CMYK colors used with the appropriate custom colors. If a custom proofing system is not available at your service bureau, it is wise to find a third party to make a custom proof.

It is also possible to make a pre-film digital proof from any CMYK printer. Because all color printers use either CMY or CMYK pigments, making an accurate pre-film proof can be tricky—if you send the file as it is to the CMYK printer, the custom colors you speci-

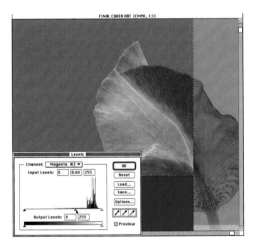

FIGURE 16:14

Using Levels, I adjusted each channel separately by choosing the desired channel from the Channel pop-up menu.

FIGURE 16:15

The Photoshop file imported into Illustrator. Illustrator's progressive color patches have been altered to match the custom Printing Inks Setup built in Photoshop, which is reflected in the appearance of the Paint Style dialog box.

fied will be replaced with CMYK color (**FIGURE 16:16**).To get an accurate proof you must convert the file to RGB and then back to CMYK using an appropriate Printing Inks Setup for the device you will be using. To make a pre-film proof:

1 Open the custom color file with the custom Printing Inks Setup loaded so that the file previews correctly and make a duplicate of the file.

2 The file must be printed from Photoshop, so if you have added elements in Illustrator, place the Illustrator file on the Photoshop file (**FIGURE 16:17**). See Chapter Thirteen, *Importing from Illustrator.*

3 Convert the file to RGB mode; its preview will not change.

4 Open Printing Inks Setup, click Load, and load

Sending the custom color file to a CMYK printer results in the custom colors being replaced with cyan and magenta.

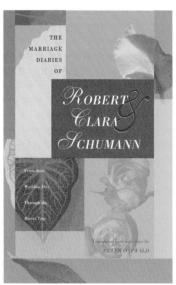

FIGURE 16:16

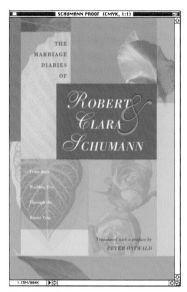

To make a pre-film proof, first place any Illustrator elements onto the Photoshop file.

FIGURE 16:17

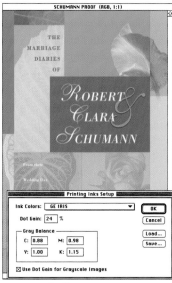

FIGURE 16:18

the printer profile you have made for the proofing device (see Chapter Fifteen, *Color Management*). Convert the file back to CMYK and send this file to the designated printer (**FIGURE 16:18**).

 It is important to make the proof file from a duplicate of the original, since once you convert from CMYK to RGB and back to CMYK, the original CMYK values are lost.

The accuracy of this proof depends on the accuracy of the initial custom Printing Inks Setup and the profile of the proofing printer. It is also possible to use custom colors that are out of gamut to CMYK, so those colors would not proof accurately off a CMYK printer. **FIGURE 16:19** shows three other book jackets printed with custom inks.

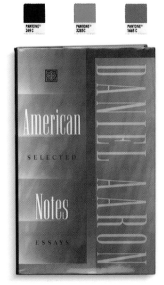

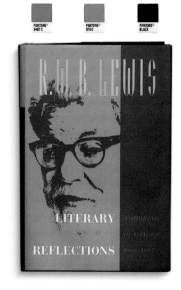

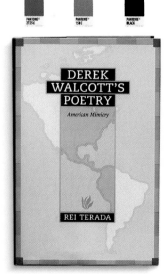

FIGURE 16:19

Three book jackets designed by Virginia Evans for Northeastern University Press using custom ink colors.

APPENDIX A

FILE FORMATS

Once you have finished a Photoshop illustration, you may want to export the artwork to a page layout or drawing program, where type or flat color can be added. Moving Photoshop art into other programs saves the time and cost of mechanically stripping the art and type together. Exporting also gives you the opportunity to use type and imagery in ways that would be impossible or too expensive to create traditionally. There are, however, some technical problems that come with exporting. This appendix covers some techniques that make the production end of output run smoothly.

You can save Photoshop art in any of more than 15 file formats for exporting to other programs and computer platforms. Three of the formats—PICT FILE, EPS, and TIFF—are useful for exporting to and printing from page layout or drawing programs. If you want to exchange files between IBM and Macintosh computers, you can use either TIFF or Photoshop format.

PICT FILE

PICT files are useful for previewing high-resolution art accurately in page layout programs and for creating templates used for guides in drawing programs (see Chapter Thirteen, *Importing from Illustrator,* FIGURES 13:15 – 13:20). Although you can print a PICT file, the quality is not adequate for final output. If your monitor displays 24 bit color, the PICT FILE format can be useful for presenting page layouts that contain high-resolution Photoshop files. After the presentation, the PICT files can be replaced with EPS files for final output. When you save a Photoshop file as a pict file, you are given resolution choices of 1, 2, 4, 8, 16, or 32 bits/pixel. This determines how many colors can be shown on screen, and is limited by the bit depth of your display (see Chapter One, *Displayed Color*). Choose 32 bits/pixel if your monitor displays 24 bit color. When you import a 32 bit PICT file into a page layout program, the preview is in 24 bit color, and looks as clear as the original Photoshop file.

EPS

Save files in the EPS format when you are exporting a Photoshop file to create composite film separations that include type and other graphic elements. Bitmap, grayscale, RGB, or CMYK images can all be saved in the EPS format.

You can export an RGB image in EPS format, but it is better to convert it to CMYK before exporting it, to take advantage of Photoshop's superior separating capabilities. The EPS format also protects your file from being altered in the page layout program to which it is exported. If you have used Photoshop's color management tools, it is important that the file's values are not adjusted by another program. When you save a CMYK file in the EPS format, you can choose from a number of options that affect the way the file is exported (FIGURE A:1). Below is an overview of the options available when you save a CMYK file in EPS format.

PREVIEW   You can determine the way Photoshop art is previewed in the program to which it is exported. If you choose None, no preview appears; 1 bit/pixel sends a black and white preview, and 8 bits/pixel sends a 256-color preview. None of these options affects the print quality of the Photoshop file. However, if the linkage is broken between the Photoshop file and the program to which it is exported, the low-resolution PICT is printed in place of the original file.

ENCODING   Always choose Binary Encoding, unless the program to which you are exporting supports only ASCII. Most programs now support Binary, which creates a file that is about half the size of an ASCII file.

INCLUDE HALFTONE SCREENS AND TRANSFER FUNCTIONS   Both of these options usually should be left unchecked. If you check Include Halftone Screens, the halftone screen frequencies and angles specified in Photoshop's Page Setup dialog box override the halftone frequency specified in the page layout program. This is particularly undesirable when you output color images as film separations. Most high-end imagesetters use proprietary screen angles that should not be changed, since they are designed to eliminate unwanted moiré patterns that can occur in an electronic separation. An instance where you would want to check Include Halftone Screens is for exporting duotones. Check with your printer to get the correct screen angles and frequencies for duotones.

If you calibrate your monitor to each output device using the methods described in Chapter Fifteen, then it is very important not to check Include Transfer Functions. Transfer functions are a way of compensating for a miscalibrated imagesetter; for example, if you specify a 35% halftone dot and the imagesetter is printing a 38% halftone dot, you can force the imagesetter to make a 35% dot by specifying a transfer function of 32%, compensating for the 3% gain. A professionally run service bureau or trade shop constantly maintains their equipment so that if you specify a 35% tint with Photoshop, the resulting film output will have a 35% halftone dot. If you check Include Transfer Functions, any transfer functions specified in Page Setup affect the separation, and the calibration adjustments that you have made may no longer be valid.

"DESKTOP COLOR SEPARATION" (5 FILES)   Checking the "Desktop Color Separation" (5 files) box saves the CMYK file as five separate files: one file for each of the CMYK separations, plus a fifth master file for placing the art in another program. If you do not check the "Desktop Color Separation" (5 files) box, the CMYK file is saved as one composite file. An advantage of the five-file format is that a low-resolution file is included that is automatically used if you proof the page on a black and white or color printer. Choose Master file: 72 pixels/inch grayscale for black and white printers, and Master file: 72 pixels/inch CMYK color for proofing on color printers. Pages that include large Photoshop files print out much faster if you include a low-resolution master file.

There are some expensive color printers that produce near continuous-tone output (they do not use halftone dots). The Canon Color Copier and the Iris Inkjet printer are the most commonly used printers of this variety. If you print from one of these printers, do not use the five-file format, because you want the high-resolution CMYK file to be printed and not the 72 pixels/inch master file that is included in the five-file format. Ask someone at your service bureau which format they prefer, composite or five-file EPS; depending on the imagesetter or program to which you are exporting, they may have a preference.

TIFF

The TIFF format can be used for printing Photoshop files from another program, but it does not offer as many options as EPS. Most drawing programs accept only EPS files, which usually print faster than TIFF files. However, TIFF files take up less disk space than EPS, and it is possible to export TIFF RGB files and let the page layout program separate the files.Do not use the tiff format if you are using Photoshop's color management tools. Many page-layout programs allow TIFF files to be modified within the program and this is not desirable if you are making final color separations in Photoshop as described in Chapter 15, *Color Management.*

APPENDIX B
EXPORTING TO ILLUSTRATOR

Once you have imported a Photoshop file into another program, maintaining the link between the Photoshop file and the page layout is important. Page layout programs usually have picture usage dialog boxes that show the current status of imported art. Adobe Illustrator does not show the status of imported art; separations must be printed from another program, so maintaining the linkages can be even more difficult. When you are ready to send an Illustrator file with placed Photoshop art to your service bureau or printer, copying the files to a transport disk will break the linkage between the Illustrator file and the placed Photoshop files. Either you can re-establish the link, or your service bureau can—it's usually safer to do it yourself.

To make sure the files are linked:

- After you move the Illustrator and Photoshop files to the disk that you are sending to your service bureau, Illustrator will still look for the placed files on your hard disk. You can move the original files to another disk and then trash the files on your hard disk. In this case, when you open the Illustrator file on the transport disk, you will be prompted to find any placed Photoshop files. As you are prompted, double-click on the appropriate Photoshop files (make sure you click on the Photoshop files that are on the transport disk). The Illustrator file opens and the link with the Photoshop files on the transport disk is made.

- Save the Illustrator file as EPS format so that it can be exported into Adobe Separator or whatever separation program will be used.

- If the file is to be output from Adobe Separator, it is not necessary to check Include Placed Images in Illustrator 5.5's EPS format dialog box.

- If the file is to be output from another third-party program (many service bureaus use Quark Xpress to separate and output Illustrator files), then you should check Include Placed Images. In this case the Photoshop files are included in the Illustrator file and the Illustrator file will become very large, so you may want to leave Include Placed Images unchecked, and ask your service bureau to resave the file including the placed images.

APPENDIX C
FASTER PHOTOSHOP

There are a number of factors beyond the raw speed of your computer that affect Photoshop's performance. Because Photoshop uses its own virtual memory scheme, the way you manage your hard disk and random access memory (RAM) affects the speed of Photoshop operations. This appendix contains some strategies for improving Photoshop's performance.

VIRTUAL MEMORY

Because you may often work on a file that is larger than your computer's available memory, Photoshop employs a method of storing the file and its copies onto your hard disk as you work. This means that as long as you have enough open space on your hard disk, you will never get an out-of-memory warning for most operations (some filters such as the Lighting Effects filter cannot use virtual memory). Unfortunately, there is a price to pay for this scheme, because reading and writing to a fast hard disk can be about about 10 times slower than having the file and its copies stored in ram. You will notice a significant increase in speed if you add memory to your computer.

Photoshop 3.0's virtual memory scheme is somewhat different from version 2.5's. The new virtual memory scheme is faster, but there are some rules you should follow to get the optimum performance from virtual memory:

- Apple's System 7.x has its own virtual memory scheme, which can conflict with Photoshop's virtual memory. Make sure that you open the system's Memory control panel and turn off Virtual Memory when you are using Photoshop.

- Make sure that you set the Disk Cache Size to the lowest setting (96K or less) and restart when using Photoshop. Increasing the Disk Cache can slow Photoshop's performance.

- With earlier versions of Photoshop you could always tell when you had run out of RAM and were using virtual memory by the activity of the disk designated as the scratch disk (the disk used for virtual memory) in the Scratch Disks submenu under Preferences. Photoshop 3.0 is often building the virtual memory space, so there can be disk activity even though virtual memory is not being used. Click and drag on the black arrow in the lower left corner of a Photoshop window and choose Scratch Disks from the pop-up menu. Now the left number in the lower left corner shows the total amount of RAM and disk space being currently used, while the number on the right shows the amount of RAM assigned to Photoshop. When the left number is larger than the right, you are using virtual memory.

MANAGING A HARD DISK   If you work on a file that overflows the available RAM, it is important to properly manage the disk that is used for virtual memory. Below are some ways to manage your hard disk and improve its performance.

- If you have more than one disk attached to your computer, you can choose either one or two of them to be used as virtual memory disks. To designate a scratch disk, choose Scratch Disks from the Preferences submenu under File. The Scratch Disks dialog box contains a pop-up menu that allows you to choose up to two scratch disks from the disks available on your system.

- If you have multiple disks available, designate the emptiest and fastest disk as the primary scratch disk. A disk's access speed is rated in milliseconds; the disk with the fastest access time should be the scratch disk.

- If possible, use an empty disk as the scratch disk. You must have at least three to five times the size of the file you are working on of combined RAM and empty disk space available, or you will run out of disk space.

- Photoshop 3.0 needs large amounts of contiguous scratch disk space even if you have lots of RAM. If you have 128 MB of RAM and only 30 MB of scratch disk, you can get an out of scratch disk message even though you are not using virtual memory.

- Defragment the scratch disk often if you also use it to store files. A defragmenting utility costs $30 to $50, and is used to reorder the files stored on the disk without reformatting the disk. Defragmenting will make all of the empty space on the disk contiguous and can improve Photoshop's virtual memory performance.

MANAGING RAM If you can avoid using virtual memory, you will notice a profound increase in Photoshop's performance. The rule of three to five times the file size also applies with RAM; if you are working on a 6 MB file, you will need 20 to 30 MB of RAM available to Photoshop, or the scratch disk will be used. Below are some tips for managing memory.

- You must have 32 bit Addressing on in the Memory control panel to access more than 8 MB of RAM. (If you are using System 7.5 make sure that Modern Memory Manager is turned on)

- If you want to take advantage of extra RAM, you must make it available to Photoshop. While you are in the finder, choose About This Macintosh from the Apple menu, and note the Largest Unused Block Size. Quit Photoshop if it is running, then highlight the Photoshop icon, choose Get Info from the finder's File menu, and change the Preferred size setting to between 1 and 2 MB less than the Largest Unused Block Size. Now, when you launch Photoshop, the amount of RAM that you designated as the Preferred size will be accessed. Windows users see Appendix E, *Photoshop for Windows*.

- Make sure that you use the most economical file size possible that still maintains the quality necessary for the job (see Chapter Four, *Image Resolution*). Not only are large files slower to work with, they are also more time-consuming to manage.

- Do not make white borders surrounding the art—white pixels take up as much memory as colored pixels.

- If you copy a large section of a high-resolution file, clear it from the clipboard after you paste it by randomly selecting a few pixels and copying them. Any art on the clipboard takes up space in memory. This is also true for Take Snapshot and Define Pattern. Once you are finished using a snapshot or pattern, select just a few pixels and define a new pattern or take a new snapshot to clear the larger images from memory.

- The preview icons that show in the Channels and Layers palettes are very useful for navigating through a Photoshop image. These previews will, however, slow the performance of Photoshop. Unless you rely on the preview icons, turn them off. Choose Palette Options from the palette's pop-up menu to turn off the previews.

- Avoid resampling your files when they have multiple layers. If possible determine the correct size and resolution of the piece before you start to work.

DISK ARRAYS

It is true that you probably can never have too much RAM, but at $40 to $50 per MB, 128 MB will cost you much more than your computer itself. An alternative to large amounts of RAM is a disk array. A disk array utilizes two fast disks and splits the data between the two disks—this is called striping. A striped disk array is usually connected to the computer via a nubus card and can be up to three times faster than a normal disk. With Photoshop 3.0's improved virtual memory scheme an empty disk array designated as the scratch disk can greatly improve Photoshop's virtual memory performance. Also, the time saving and opening large files will be drastically cut.

QUICK EDIT

A new feature of Photoshop 3.0 is Quick Edit. Quick Edit allows you to edit part of an image without actually opening the entire file. To use Quick Edit:

1 Choose Quick Edit from the Acquire submenu under Edit.

2 You can choose any file in Photoshop 2.0 format to edit. This means you can't work on a file with layers.

3 When you choose a file from the directory, the Quick Edit dialog appears with a preview of the file. Clicking and dragging on the preview pulls out a marquee which designates the part of the image which will be opened—you can open a 2 MB piece of a 50 MB file. You can also check the Grid box and a grid will appear over the preview—click on the grid to designate which part of the image will be opened.

4 Click OK to open the designated part of the file. Make the desired changes and choose Quick Edit Save from the Export submenu under File. The edited piece is copied back to the original file.

APPENDIX D
SHORTCUTS

Here is a list of tips and shortcuts which can save you time when using Photoshop:

- When any painting tool is selected typing a number adjusts the tool's opacity. Type 1 to get 10%, 2 to get 20%, and so on.

- If any tool but a painting tool is selected and there is a layer or floating selection targeted, then typing a number adjusts the layer's opacity.

- Holding down the Option key when using the Eraser reverts the erased part of the image to the last saved version of the file.

- Use Take Snapshot or Define Pattern to apply color corrections or filters with the paint tools. See FIGURES 8:2 – 10.

- Option+Delete fills the selected area with the foreground color. Shift+Delete opens the Fill dialog box.

- When any selection tool is selected, hold down Option+Command and drag to move the selection marquee, press the arrow keys to move the marquee in 1 pixel increments.

- Holding down the Command key while the Type tool is selected and there is a floating selection, turns the Type tool into a Lasso. Any part of the floating selection which is intersected with the Lasso is pasted down, rather than deleted as is the case if the Lasso tool is selected.

- You can skip cutting and pasting by dragging and dropping selections from one window to another. To drag a selected area into another window, a selection tool, or the Type tool must be active. If another tool is active hold down the Command key before dragging.

- There are a number of ways to load a channel mask as a selection without choosing Load Selection from the Select menu. See page 130.

- Command+Option+T selects the non-transparent areas of the targeted layer.

- If the are no active selections in a document, hold down the Option key while choosing Apply image to add Result to the dialog box. See FIGURE 14:13.

- You can quickly select a tool by pressing a letter on the keyboard. See FIGURE 3:11.

- There is not a page guide function in Photoshop, but you can easily make guides in an additional channel which can be viewed with the document. See FIGURES 11:36 – 39.

- Double-click the Hand tool to instantly fit the entire image into the display area.

- Double-click the Zoom tool to instantly set the monitor to image ratio to 1:1.

- Clicking and dragging on an image with Command+Spacebar pressed selects an area that is magnified to fill the window or screen.

- Type Command++ or Command+- to zoom in or out of an image. Adding the Option key zooms to the maximum or minimum magnifications.

- You can use the Cropping tool to resize or resample an image in one step. See FIGURE 5:13.

- To change a Background to a Layer which can have transparency, double-click Background in the Layers palette, click OK, and the Background becomes Layer 0.

- You can change the default settings of the Screen or Transfer functions in Page Setup. Choose Page Setup, click Screen or Transfer, adjust the dialog box to the desired settings. Hold down the Option key and the Save button becomes >Default, click >Default and the current settings are saved as the new default.

- Holding down the Option key while choosing Calculations reduces the size of the dialog box which can be useful with smaller monitors.

- Press the Tab key to hide the tool box and palettes. If you are using the Pen tool, press T to show an active path. Press Option+Tab to hide only the tool box.

- Option+Command+M opens the Curves dialog box with the last applied curve loaded.

- When a dialog box is open, press the up or down arrow keys to increase or decrease the dialog box value by 1 unit increments. Add the Shift key to make the change in 10 unit increments.

APPENDIX E

PHOTOSHOP FOR WINDOWS

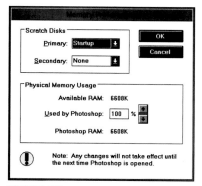

FIGURE E:1

I have made all of the screen captures for this book from the Macintosh version of Photoshop, and the operating system references in the text are to Apple's System 7; however, a Windows user should have little difficulty applying the described techniques using the Windows version of Photoshop. Below is a list of the few differences between the programs:

KEY COMMANDS Under Windows the keyboard shortcuts for the menu items are different from the Macintosh version. Windows users should substitute the Alt key for Option, and the Ctrl key for Command.

MEMORY USAGE The amount of memory (RAM) that is available to Photoshop is assigned from within Photoshop under Windows. To make more or less memory available to Photoshop, choose Memory from the Preferences submenu under File (**FIGURE E:1**). The dialog box lets you assign which disk or disks will be used as Scratch Disks (virtual memory) and what percentage of available RAM will be used by Photoshop. To change the amount of ram available to Photoshop adjust the percentage under Physical Memory Usage and restart Photoshop.

PERMANENT SWAP FILE The Windows permanent swap file must be at least equal to the amount of RAM available before Windows loads in order for Photoshop to run correctly.

MONITOR CALIBRATION Windows users can adjust their monitor's gamma and white point from within the Monitor Setup preference dialog box (**FIGURE E:2**). This feature replaces the Gamma Control Panel described on page 28 for the Macintosh. Click on the Calibrate button to access a dialog which lets you change the gamma and white point of Photoshop files. Once you have decided on a gamma and white point setting refer to page 212 before adjusting the Monitor Setup preferences.

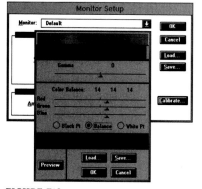

FIGURE E:2

PRODUCTION NOTES

This book was produced using a Power Macintosh 7100 with 40MB of RAM and a 1 gigabyte FWB SledgeHammer disk array. A 650 MB Ricoh optical drive was used for storage and transportation of the high resolution files. Unless otherwise noted, all of the scanning for this book was done using relatively inexpensive desktop scanners—a Microtek 300z flatbed, and a Nikon LS-3500 slide scanner. The software used for production were: QuarkXpress 3.3, Adobe Illustrator 5.5, Adobe Photoshop 3.0, QuicKeys 3.0, and Flash-it 3.0.2. QuarkXpress was used for word processing and page layout. Photoshop and Illustrator were used to create the illustrations, and Flash-it was used for capturing screens.

Initial illustrations and screen captures were saved in RGB mode as Photoshop 3.0 format, and stored on 650MB removable optical disks. As the artwork was created, a low resolution, black-and-white, bitmapped version of each illustration was saved as EPS format into a separate folder. The low resolution files had the same name as the corresponding high resolution files, and were used for placement in the page layout and proofing. QuicKeys was used to automate this process.

When the page layout was complete the high resolution, RGB Photoshop files were converted to CMYK EPS files. Before making the conversions to CMYK I created a Printing Inks Setup based on the printing of the first edition of this book (see page 215). The custom Printing Inks Setup compensated for the extra dot gain that would occur on the high speed web press used to print this book. When the high resolution files were complete, the low resolution files were trashed, and Quark's Picture Usage feature was used to automatically place the high resolution files. The finished files were then proofed from a Canon Color Copier to check the placement of the high resolution images. Film separations were output as imposed signatures from an AGFA SelectSet 7000 imagesetter, with a MultiStar 600Adobe PostScript Level 2 RIP.

INDEX

COLOPHON

Designer Photoshop was set in Utopia, an Adobe
Original typeface family designed by Robert Slimbach
at Adobe Systems. The captions and notes were set in
Myriad, a multiple master typeface designed by Robert
Slimbach and Carol Twombly. The prepress, printing,
and binding was done by R.R. Donnelley & Sons.
The book was designed by Virginia Evans.
Unless otherwise credited all illustrations
and photography are by the author.